HBR Guide to
Collaborative
Teams

Harvard Business Review Guides

Arm yourself with the advice you need to succeed on the job, from the most trusted brand in business. Packed with how-to essentials from leading experts, the HBR Guides provide smart answers to your most pressing work challenges.

The titles include:

HBR Guide for Women at Work

HBR Guide to Beating Burnout

HBR Guide to Being More Productive

HBR Guide to Better Business Writing

HBR Guide to Building Your Business Case

HBR Guide to Buying a Small Business

HBR Guide to Changing Your Career

HBR Guide to Coaching Employees

HBR Guide to Collaborative Teams

HBR Guide to Data Analytics Basics for Managers

HBR Guide to Dealing with Conflict

HBR Guide to Delivering Effective Feedback

HBR Guide to Emotional Intelligence

HBR Guide to Finance Basics for Managers

HBR Guide to Getting the Mentoring You Need

HBR Guide to Getting the Right Job

HBR Guide to Getting the Right Work Done

HBR Guide to Leading Teams

HBR Guide to Making Better Decisions

HBR Guide to Making Every Meeting Matter

HBR Guide to Managing Strategic Initiatives

HBR Guide to Managing Stress at Work

HBR Guide to Managing Up and Across

HBR Guide to Motivating People

HBR Guide to Negotiating

HBR Guide to Networking

HBR Guide to Office Politics

HBR Guide to Performance Management

HBR Guide to Persuasive Presentations

HBR Guide to Project Management

HBR Guide to Remote Work

HBR Guide to Setting Your Strategy

HBR Guide to Thinking Strategically

HBR Guide to Work-Life Balance

HBR Guide to Your Professional Growth

HBR Guide to
Collaborative Teams

HARVARD BUSINESS REVIEW PRESS

Boston, Massachusetts

Copyright 2021 Harvard Business School Publishing Corporation

Cataloging-in-Publication data is forthcoming.
ISBN: 978-1-64782-089-3
eISBN: 978-1-64782-090-9

The paper used in this publication meets the requirements of the American National Standard for Permanence of Paper for Publications and Documents in Libraries and Archives Z39.48-1992.

What You'll Learn

More and more, individuals in organizations are being asked to work together to accomplish important projects and meet key objectives. But effective collaboration is no easy task. From navigating competing priorities to simply finding time for team members to meet, any number of obstacles can slow down productivity or even lead to failure. Getting all members of a cross-functional team on the same page, and working toward the same goal, is far easier said than done.

Collaboration is a skill that many companies expect of their employees but rarely train them in. Building a diverse team, ensuring everyone can work together smoothly, setting norms around communication and decision making, and proactively resolving conflicts all tend to be left to team leaders—who may not even have formal authority over the people they're leading. It's no wonder collaboration can feel like an uphill struggle. But it doesn't have to.

Whether you're leading a collaborative team for the first time or you've worked on cross-functional initiatives for years, this guide will help you manage challenges and solve problems so your projects reach successful outcomes. You'll learn how to:

- Find the right mix of skills and personalities for your project

- Lead and motivate people you don't have authority over

- Ensure all team members understand their roles and responsibilities

- Manage a high-powered group of "A" players

- Create the psychological safety people need to do their best work

- Make decisions as a group—even when team members disagree

- Solve turf wars and interpersonal conflicts

- Collaborate effectively across locations and zones

- Work productively with colleagues you don't get along with

- Help team members execute on goals

- Set the conditions for agile teamwork

Contents

Introduction   1

Why Collaboration Is So Hard

*To work together well, we need to embrace
our differences.*

BY JEFF WEISS

SECTION ONE

Making Yourself Collaboration-Ready

1. Exerting Influence Without Authority   9

   *To lead people who don't report to you,
   try lateral leadership.*

   BY LAUREN KELLER JOHNSON

2. To Improve Your Team, First Work   17
   on Yourself

   You need three specific capabilities.

   BY JENNIFER PORTER

3. Collaboration Without Burnout   25

   Figure out where you add the most value.

   BY ROB CROSS, SCOTT TAYLOR, AND DEB ZEHNER

Contents

SECTION TWO

Building the Team

4. Great Teams Are About Personalities,   39
   Not Just Skills
   Here's how to get the right mix.
   BY DAVE WINSBOROUGH AND TOMAS
   CHAMORRO-PREMUZIC

5. Six Ways to Convince Someone to   47
   Collaborate with You
   Think about what you can offer them
   in return.
   BY DORIE CLARK

6. Making Star Teams Out of Star Players   55
   There's a right way and a wrong way to
   organize them.
   BY MICHAEL MANKINS, ALAN BIRD, AND JAMES ROOT

7. Ensuring Agile Teams Can Work Together   65
   Nurturing internal networks can lead to
   better outcomes.
   BY ALIA CROCKER, ROB CROSS, AND HEIDI K. GARDNER

SECTION THREE

Being Productive as a Team

8. High-Performing Teams Need   79
   Psychological Safety
   Here's how to create it.
   BY LAURA DELIZONNA

9. **The Best Teams Have Clearly Defined Roles**   87

   Fuzzy responsibilities are bad for collaboration.

   BY TAMMY ERICKSON

10. **Helping Teams with Different Subcultures to Collaborate**   91

   Every company has many cultures.

   BY ROGER SCHWARZ

11. **Get Your Team to Do What It Says It's Going to Do**   97

   "If-then planning" is the key.

   BY HEIDI GRANT

12. **Don't Let Teamwork Get in the Way of Agility**   111

   Each project stage needs the right amount of teamwork.

   BY ELAINE D. PULAKOS AND ROBERT B. (ROB) KAISER

13. **How to Motivate Your Problem People**   121

   The most intractable people take up the most time and energy.

   BY NIGEL NICHOLSON

SECTION FOUR

Communicating and Making Decisions

14. **Cracking the Code of Sustained Collaboration**   147

   Six tools for training people to work together better.

   BY FRANCESCA GINO

15. **Seven Strategies for Better Group Decision Making**   165

    Keep the group small and diverse.

    BY TORBEN EMMERLING AND DUNCAN ROODERS

16. **A Good Meeting Needs a Clear Decision-Making Process**   171

    Before you start, agree on how it will end.

    BY BOB FRISCH AND CARY GREENE

17. **Four Tips for Effective Virtual Collaboration**   175

    Be strategic about meetings and communication.

    BY ELIZABETH GRACE SAUNDERS

18. **If Your Team Agrees on Everything, Working Together Is Pointless**   183

    Constructive conflict is good for creativity.

    BY LIANE DAVEY

SECTION FIVE

Navigating Conflicts and Power Struggles

19. **How to Permanently Resolve Cross-Department Rivalries**   191

    Four questions to start getting on the same page.

    BY RON CARUCCI

20. **Navigating a Turf War at Work**   197

    Check your mindset, and focus on the larger goal.

    BY AMY GALLO

21. **How to Handle a Disagreement on Your Team**   207

Be a mediator, not a boss.

BY JEANNE BRETT AND STEPHEN B. GOLDBERG

22. **Collaborating with People You Don't Like**   217

You can still have a productive relationship.

BY MARK D. NEVINS

Index   **223**

Why Collaboration Is So Hard

by Jeff Weiss

For most of us, getting work done requires skilled collaboration. Whether we are designing, producing, selling, solving, changing, or implementing, we need to work with others. But putting a group of talented, hardworking people together and telling them to execute on a project is generally not a recipe for success. To achieve the full value of collaboration, leaders need to enable members of the team to manage their differences.

It's challenging enough to collaborate with likeminded teammates, people you know and trust. Working with colleagues in other departments, functions, or business units—or a key supplier, customer, or partner—is considerably more difficult. No matter how well intended everyone is, conflicting goals, incentives, mental models, and a long list of other potential obstacles can keep a problem from being solved or a task completed, never mind done creatively and efficiently.

For over three decades, I have had the privilege of seeing complex collaborations up close. I've studied them, written and taught on how to manage them, advised on them, and even led them, in areas ranging from business to academia to the military. And through this, I've seen clearly why certain teams are extraordinarily successful, while others get little done and their efforts end in disaster.

Those great successes are partly a result of having the right people with the right knowledge, skills, and tools. Even more important, however, is the team's ability to build relationships, communicate, manage conflict, and, especially, make good use of their many differences. But none of this happens without individuals who can guide their teams through the challenges of collaboration. How to do that is the focus of this book.

The Power of Diverse Voices

Consider three situations we face in our daily work:

- Bringing together various forms of expertise to solve a problem, design something new, or develop a robust proposal

- Combining multiple perspectives to share a recommendation, plan, or solution

- Using many different ways of thinking and types of experience to fully understand a challenge, see opportunities and threats in new ways, or catalyze innovation

Each of these requires assembling and working with people across functions and often across organizations— people with real *differences*. Yet while the strength of collaboration is rooted in that diversity of perspectives, far too often we ignore it or wish it away. As a seasoned senior leader once shared with me, echoing many of my clients and colleagues over time, "We brought all of these people together to leverage our different capabilities, ways of thinking, and expertise, and within a month, I find myself wishing they'd just be more like I am."

This should be no surprise. It takes real effort to manage differences, and when they are not managed well (as is the case all too often), the result is conflict, miscommunication, and wasted time. This happens not just once but over and over again, as the team tries to define the problem being addressed, diagnose and approach it, set timelines and roles, and design the plan or solution.

Moreover, leaders who mismanage differences lose out on what they bring to the table. The varying expertise and objectives of people from various functions forces us to grapple with intentional, necessary business tensions in problem solving. Think of a collaboration among finance, legal, sales, engineering, and quality departments. Such a team could drive innovation while also managing risk; design outstanding products while also managing cost; and balance speed and quality with safety, pricing, and customer satisfaction—all at the same time. Drawing on differing perspectives helps teams come up with a solution that no one function could create on its own and ensure that solution meets the needs of diverse constituents.

Given the critical need to manage diverse viewpoints and skill sets, it should be no surprise that there are some telltale signs of highly effective cross-functional teams. On those teams, we repeatedly hear colleagues asking a particular set of questions:

- **Why?** For what purpose are you suggesting that, based on what interests, shaped by what objectives?

- **Could you help me understand?** What is the reasoning path—the story from your point of view— that leads you to that interpretation, perception, conclusion?

- **What assumptions are we making?** What do we each think we know about the situation, what is possible, what is each other's intent?

- **What other ways might we view or solve this?** What other possibilities might exist, how else could we explain or achieve this, what other creative solutions might we explore?

- **What is the basis for this decision?** What objective criteria could help us determine what we should do, would provide a sense of fairness, could enable us to explain our decision?

Colleagues who collaborate well pose these questions to one another, probe for answers, ensure they have understood, and use what they uncover to tackle the situation at hand. They employ well-understood differences as grist for creative, side-by-side problem-solving. With newfound knowledge and appreciation of one another, they are able to work together *because* of their differences, not in spite of them.

Of course, the effective collaboration highlighted here does not just emerge. It comes from leaders and team members who know how challenging this kind of collaboration can be and who take a disciplined approach to supporting it. These individuals make it their job to model asking the questions and exhibiting the behaviors I've described, to spot and diagnose breakdowns in them, and to coach those around them to do the same. And, as a result, those collaborating begin to think and work differently. They seek to understand differences, rather than being resentful of them, and use them to fuel the collaboration.

What This Book Will Do

As you will see in the chapters that follow, successful collaborators focus as much on *how* they and others work together as on *what* they are trying to solve or produce. Whether you're leading a team of individuals from across the organization (or across the globe) or have recently been asked to join a diverse team, you will learn the essential skills to ensure a productive—and even energizing—collaboration. You'll learn to prepare yourself for collaborative projects; build a team that includes a variety of skills, personalities, and viewpoints; ensure execution on shared goals; establish communication and decision-making norms; and navigate turf wars, power struggles, and other forms of conflict within your team.

Leaders who master these skills will not only lead their teams to better results. They'll also help to make working together a lot more fun and fulfilling.

Jeff Weiss is the chief strategy and transformation officer of the Mass General Brigham health system. He is a longtime contributor to *Harvard Business Review* on topics such as cross-matrix collaboration, conflict management, negotiation, and managing partnerships, and is the author of the *HBR Guide to Negotiation*.

Making Yourself Collaboration-Ready

CHAPTER 1

Exerting Influence Without Authority

by Lauren Keller Johnson

Congratulations—you've been asked to lead a change initiative! But there's a catch—its success hinges on the cooperation of several people across your organization over whom you have no formal authority.

If you're like most managers, you're facing this sort of challenge more often these days because of flatter management structures, outsourcing, and virtual teams. For those reasons, a greater number of managers now need to get things done through peers inside and outside their organizations. In this age of heightened business complexity, moreover, change itself has grown increasingly

---

Adapted from content posted on hbr.org, February 28, 2008.

complicated. A majority of change initiatives now involve multiple functions within and even between companies, and many such efforts encompass an entire firm.
New kinds of partnerships and alliances have emerged
as well, and they require managers to exercise influence
over peers from the other companies.

In such circumstances, command-and-control leadership—the "I leader, you follower" approach—doesn't
get you very far. According to Jay A. Conger, professor of organizational behavior at the London Business
School and formerly the executive director of the University of Southern California's Leadership Institute,
managers and executives at all levels must use a more
lateral style of leadership.

Why Lateral Leadership?

Lateral leadership, Conger says, counts among a manager's most essential skills and comprises a constellation
of capabilities—from networking and coalition building
to persuading and negotiating.

Though honing these skills takes time and patience,
the payoff is worth it. That initiative you're championing will stand a far better chance of being implemented
quickly. You'll gain access to the resources you need to
carry out the effort. You'll see doors swing open freely to
the key players whose cooperation you need most. And
perhaps most important, you'll achieve the central purpose of managerial work: getting things done through
other people—and catalyzing valuable change for your
organization.

A constellation of capabilities

So how do you begin mastering the skills that constitute lateral leadership? Conger recommends focusing
on four closely interconnected and mutually reinforcing
capabilities.

Networking

Cultivate a broad network of relationships with the
people inside and outside your company whose support you need to carry out your initiatives. If networking doesn't come naturally to you, create a personal dis-
cipline through which to acquire this capability. Conger
maintains that "certain people are portals to other people—they can connect you to more and bigger networks.
You need to build relationships with these individuals in
particular."

Constructive persuasion and negotiation

Too many managers, Conger says, wrongly view persuasion and negotiation as tools for manipulation. Conducted with an eye toward mutual benefit, they can
vastly enhance your influence.

To make persuasion and negotiation constructive
rather than manipulative, view the person you're dealing
with as a peer instead of a "target." Take courses and read
books on these subjects to hone your skills. And find a
seasoned colleague within the company who can serve as
a confidant and brainstorming partner.

Consultation

Take time to visit the people whose buy-in you need. Ask their opinions about the initiative you're championing. Get their ideas as well as their reactions to your ideas.

Too many managers, Conger says, rush to define a series of steps that they believe constitutes the right way to carry out their initiative. They then circulate around the company and try to impose their solution on others—mistakenly believing that they're engaging in productive consultation.

The result? Resistance and bickering over process details. "You'll get far better results," Conger says, "if you commit to and advocate the desired outcome but invite peers to participate in defining the process for achieving that outcome."

Coalition building

It's a fact of human nature that several people who are collectively advocating an idea exert more influence than a lone proponent. For this reason, coalition building plays a vital role in lateral leadership. By building coalitions, Conger explains, you gather influential people together to form "a single body of authority."

To assemble a powerful coalition, begin by asking yourself who's most likely to be affected by the change you're proposing. Whose "blessing" do you need—whether in the form of political support or access to important resources or individuals? Whose buy-in is crucial to your initiative's success?

The challenges of lateral leadership

Though lateral leadership consists of several concrete, interrelated skills, many managers cannot easily master those capabilities. For one thing, Conger points out, they're often so focused on their own functional silo that they don't know who beyond their own internal group should be included in their networking and coalition-building efforts.

To combat this "functional focus," take time to find out who makes things happen in your organization. Whom do people go to for advice and support? And who tends to throw up roadblocks to new ideas and changes? You won't find the answers to these questions in the organizational chart. As Conger says, you gain a sense of these things through informal contact and casual get-togethers with colleagues throughout the company.

In addition to focusing too closely on their own function, managers experience intense pressure to grapple with what they see as responsibilities more urgent than building relationships. After all, many of them are rewarded for producing concrete, short-term results, Conger notes, whereas investments in lateral leadership "capital" can take time and patience—and often the dividends don't come until much later.

So how do you reconcile the need to produce in the short run with the equally important need to lay the groundwork for productive collaboration in the long run? Conger recommends dedicating a specific amount of time each day or week to sharpening your lateral leadership skills. For example, commit to having lunch each Thursday with a different person inside or outside your organization whom you don't know well but who may play an important role in a project you'll be leading.

Conger also recommends getting to know influential people before starting to work with them on a project. For instance, suppose you'll be leading a project that will involve managers from several other functions and you've scheduled a formal kickoff meeting in a month. Seek out those managers in the weeks leading up to the meeting and ask them for their thoughts about the upcoming project.

Creating the right environment

Considering the increasing need for lateral leadership—and its unmistakable benefits—you might assume that companies are moving energetically to train managers in this important area. But, Conger notes, that isn't the case.

To be sure, many firms offer courses on influence, circulate articles on various aspects of lateral leadership, and establish mentoring programs designed to help managers identify and access "portals" quickly. But formal training and mentoring efforts can have mixed results, Conger warns.

Why? "Successful lateral leadership grows out of positive chemistry between people. You can't predict or control the natural affinity people have for one another—that glue that makes relationships of mutual influence possible."

Rather than "matching people up" through a formal mentoring program, companies have far more success by creating opportunities for people to mingle—and then letting them forge mentoring and networking relationships on their own. Conferences, seminars, and company-sponsored social events provide opportunities for people to get to know peers with whom they might not otherwise interact.

Chemistry becomes even more important, Conger adds, in virtual teams. In these increasingly common work groups, members have few chances to meet face-to-face and engage in the "sizing up" that humans do instinctively. Without these nonverbal exchanges, people can't build the trust that makes lateral leadership possible. Thus, people on virtual teams must be particularly intentional about their networking. Face-to-face meetings—even if they require expensive travel—are often well worth the cost. Lunches and other casual social gatherings can further cement working relationships. If you can't travel or meet in person, seek out ways to connect with people remotely, whether it's a virtual coffee break or just a simple phone call.

As the business landscape continues to shift, companies will need managers who can exercise lateral leadership with increasing skill and confidence. But because many firms still don't invest explicitly in cultivating this talent throughout their workforces, managers would do well to take the initiative themselves.

Lauren Keller Johnson is a New Hampshire–based business writer.

CHAPTER 2

To Improve Your Team, First Work on Yourself

by Jennifer Porter

A colleague and I were recently meeting with a CEO and his leadership team, observing them as they discussed how to improve their annual planning process. As the team of 10 explored their current process, the conversation got heated. The team had been talking for 45 minutes, but it wasn't clear who was leading the discussion or what their objectives were. Many comments were off-topic, and they were not getting closer to answers.

Adapted from content posted on hbr.org, January 29, 2019 (product #H04RGC).

We paused the meeting and posed this question: How are you reacting to this conversation and what *in you* is causing your reaction?

We were met with blank stares. They asked us to repeat the question, seemingly surprised that we had asked them to take responsibility for their reactions. Surely, we had meant to ask them what everyone *else* was doing wrong in the conversation, right?

Leaders and teammates often tell us that their team is "dysfunctional" (their word, not ours) and ask us to help identify and fix the issue. When we dig deeper and ask them to describe what they are observing in detail, we typically hear that certain team members are problematic and need to change their behavior. We also hear vague statements about "them" (everyone else) not knowing how to operate effectively. As experienced team development practitioners, we know that these are not accurate or helpful assessments of the situation.

Teams are complex systems of individuals with different preferences, skills, experiences, perspectives, and habits.[1] The odds of improving that complex system in a meaningful and sustainable way are higher if every team member—including the leader—learns to master these three foundational capabilities: internal self-awareness, external self-awareness, and personal accountability.

Internal Self-Awareness

I once asked an executive I was coaching how he was feeling about a challenging situation. He replied, "You mean my emotions? I'm an engineer and I don't think about emotions." He then changed the subject.

This executive lacked internal self-awareness.

Internal self-awareness involves understanding your feelings, beliefs, and values—your inner narrative. When we don't understand ourselves, we are more likely to succumb to the fundamental attribution error of believing that the behaviors of others are the result of negative intent or character ("he was late because he does not care") and believing that our own behaviors are caused by circumstance ("I was late because of traffic"). Teammates with low internal self-awareness typically see their beliefs and values as "the truth," as opposed to what is true *for them* based on their feelings and past experiences. They can fail to recognize that others may have equally valid perspectives.

Let's look at another example: Manuel, a low internal self-awareness leader, and his colleague, Tara. In a product planning meeting, Tara, a big-picture thinker, says, "We need to think of this plan in the context of our broader strategy." Manuel, an execution-focused leader, has an unconscious reaction of anger and frustration. He would rather focus on the detailed plan and the execution. But rather than recognizing his different thinking style as the cause of his discomfort and the root of his belief that strategy is unimportant, he concludes privately that Tara doesn't understand the situation, is annoying, and is not the right person for this project. He later tells another colleague she should be taken off the team.

This is a loss for everyone. Tara is misunderstood, devalued, and possibly dismissed. Manuel doesn't broaden his perspective or learn how to operate with people who think differently than he does.

The good news is that internal self-awareness can be learned. To start, you—as a leader of the team or a team-mate—can pause, reflect, and consider your responses to these questions when you find yourself in challenging or emotionally charged scenarios.

- What emotions am I experiencing?

- What am I assuming about another person or the situation?

- What are the facts versus my interpretations?

- What are my core values, and how might they be impacting my reactions?

If you take the time to consider your responses and resist the impulse to rush to an answer, you can learn a great deal about yourself. As William Deresiewicz, author of *Solitude and Leadership,* said in an address at West Point, "[The] first thought is never [the] best thought."

External Self-Awareness

External self-awareness involves understanding how our words and actions impact others. Most of the leaders and teammates we work with have no idea how their behaviors are impacting their colleagues. As a result, it's difficult for them to recognize and leverage the strengths that make them a productive teammate, as well as identify and correct behaviors that negatively impact the team. Without this knowledge, they can't improve.

One way to start building external self-awareness is to observe others' reactions during discussions. Did someone raise their voice? Stop talking? Gesture? Sit back from the table? Smile? You can collect some valuable information this way. You should also be mindful of the fact that you will reach some inaccurate conclusions. In these situations, remember that you are *interpreting* why colleagues react the way they do, and those interpretations will be influenced by your personal beliefs and experiences. Paying attention to your internal self-awareness and considering how you reached your initial conclusions will help.

A more direct approach is to ask teammates for specific, straightforward feedback:

- What am I doing in team meetings that is helpful?

- What am I doing that is not helpful?

- If you could change one part of how I interact with the team, what would it be?

This may feel risky and uncomfortable, but it's the only way you can get accurate data about the impact of your words and actions.

In terms of timing, you should carefully assess whether it is additive to the discussion at hand to ask for feedback in the moment, or whether it is better to ask later. For example, in a one-on-one conversation with a trusted colleague, it's probably OK to pause and ask. However, in a big team meeting, pausing the conversation to get personal feedback can be disruptive to what your team is trying to accomplish.

Personal Accountability

When we think of accountability, we typically think of holding others accountable. But the most effective leaders and teammates are more focused on holding *themselves* accountable.

Like self-awareness, this sounds easy, though it rarely is. When confronted with a challenge or discomfort, many of us have established unhealthy patterns: blaming or criticizing others, defending ourselves, feigning confusion, or avoiding the issue altogether.

If a team is not working well together, it's highly likely that every team member is contributing to the difficulty in some way, and each of them could be taking personal accountability to make the team more effective.

To be a personally accountable leader or teammate, you need to take these steps:

1. Recognize when there is a problem. Sometimes this is the hardest part because we'd rather look away or talk about how busy we are instead. Resist the urge to do so.

2. Accept that you are part of the problem. You are absolutely contributing to the situation.

3. Take personal responsibility for solving the problem.

4. Stick with it until the problem is completely solved.

Going back to the example of Manuel—if he were practicing personal accountability, he would have first recognized that he had some conflict with Tara that was impacting the team's ability to create a solid plan. He would have then had the mindset to accept that he was contributing to the conflict, committed to working on a more productive relationship with Tara, and avoided the temptation to jump to conclusions and talk behind her back.

Most teams we work with learn to operate more effectively by building and strengthening these three capabilities over time. Changing how we process information and respond requires not just learning these new skills, but also demonstrating them long enough to form new habits. Effective teammates believe that, sometimes, you have to go slow to go fast. They invest the time and energy needed to build these foundational skills, so they can be better at tackling the difficult business opportunities and challenges that they face.

Jennifer Porter is the managing partner of The Boda Group, a leadership and team development firm. She is a graduate of Bates College and the Stanford Graduate School of Business, an experienced operations executive, and an executive and team coach.

NOTES

1. Eleftheria Vasileiadou, "Research Teams as Complex Systems: Implications for Knowledge Management," *Knowledge Management Research & Practice* 10 (2012): 118–127.

CHAPTER 3

Collaboration Without Burnout

by Rob Cross, Scott Taylor, and Deb Zehner

"So many different people can get to you through different channels, and the pressure is enormous."

"Constant email, international travel, calls at all hours— I was exhausted. The collaborative demands eventually wore me down."

"I always felt I had to do more, go further, save the day. I would become people's life raft and then almost drown."

These are the voices of collaborative overload.

As organizations become more global, adopt matrixed structures, offer increasingly complex products

---

Adapted from an article in *Harvard Business Review*, July–August 2018 (product #R1804L).

and services, and enable 24/7 communication, they are requiring employees to collaborate with more internal colleagues and external contacts than ever before. According to research from Connected Commons, most managers now spend 85% or more of their work time on email, in meetings, and on the phone, and the demand for such activities has jumped by 50% over the past decade. Companies benefit, of course: Faster innovation and more-seamless client service are two by-products of greater collaboration. But along with all this comes significantly less time for focused individual work, careful reflection, and sound decision making. A 2016 HBR article coauthored by one of us dubbed this destructive phenomenon *collaborative overload* and suggested ways that organizations might combat it.

Over the past few years we've conducted further research—both quantitative and qualitative—to better understand the problem and uncover solutions that individuals can implement on their own. Working with 20 global organizations in diverse fields (software, consumer products, professional services, manufacturing, and life sciences), we started by creating models of employees' collaborations and considering the effect of those interactions on engagement, performance, and voluntary attrition. We then used network analyses to identify efficient collaborators—people who work productively with a wide variety of others but use the least amount of their own and their colleagues' time—and interviewed 200 of them (100 men and 100 women) about their working lives. We learned a great deal about how overload happens and what leaders must do to avoid it so that they can continue to thrive.

Not surprisingly, we found that always-on work cultures, encroaching technology, demanding bosses, difficult clients, and inefficient coworkers were a big part of the problem, and most of those challenges do require organizational solutions. But we discovered in many cases that external time sinks were matched by another enemy: individuals' own mindsets and habits. Fortunately, people can overcome those obstacles themselves, right away, with some strategic self-management.

We uncovered best practices in three broad categories: *beliefs* (understanding why we take on too much); *role, schedule, and network* (eliminating unnecessary collaboration to make time for work that is aligned with professional aspirations and personal values); and *behavior* (ensuring that necessary or desired collaborative work is as productive as possible). Not all our recommendations will suit everyone: People's needs differ by personality, hierarchical level, and work context. But we found that when the people we studied took action on just four or five of them, they were able to claw back 18% to 24% of their collaborative time.

Two Types of Overload

Collaborative overload generally occurs in either a surge or a slow burn. A surge can result from a promotion, a request from a boss or a colleague to take on or help out with a project, or the desire to jump into an "extracurricular" work activity because you feel obligated or don't want to miss out. Consider Mike, an insurance company executive who was already managing multiple projects— one of which had his entire team working day and night to turn around a struggling segment of the business.

When his boss asked him to help create a new unit that would allow the company to present a single face to the market, he felt he couldn't say no. It was a great development opportunity—to which his skills were perfectly suited—and it offered prime exposure to senior management. Yet he couldn't abandon his existing team in the midst of its work. So he decided to do both jobs at once.

A slow burn is more insidious and occurs through incremental increases in the volume, diversity, and pace of collaborative demands over time, as personal effectiveness leads to larger networks and greater scope of responsibilities. Go-to people in organizations suffer from this type of overload. As we gain experience, we often tend to take on more work, and our identities start to become intertwined with accomplishment, helping, or being in the know. We tend not to question what we are doing as we add tasks or work late into the night on email. And, of course, our colleagues welcome these tendencies; as we gain reputations for competence and responsiveness, people in our networks bring us more work and requests. Ellen, an 18-year veteran of a *Fortune* 100 technology company, is a case in point. She was fiercely driven and took pride in her ability to help colleagues, solve problems, and cut through bureaucracy to get things done. Eventually, however, she felt weighed down by a list of projects and commitments that were "beyond the realm of doable."

Though Mike's and Ellen's situations are different, our research suggests that the solutions to their and others' overload problems are similar. They cannot continue to work the same way they always have and remain effective. They need to take better charge of their working lives.

Why We Take On Too Much

The first step in combating collaborative overload is to recognize how much of it is driven by your own desire to maintain a reputation as a helpful, knowledgeable, or influential colleague or to avoid the anxiety that stems from ceding control over or declining to participate in group work. For example, someone who engages in the entire life cycle of a small project, beyond the time when the need for her expertise has passed, might pride herself on supporting teammates and ensuring a high-quality result. But that's not the kind of collaboration that makes a difference over the long term; indeed, too much of it will prevent her from doing more-important work.

Knowing why you accept collaborative work—above and beyond what your manager and your company demand—is how you begin to combat overload. When we counsel executives, we ask them to reflect on the specific identity-based triggers that most often lead them into overload. For example: Do you crave the feeling of accomplishment that comes from ticking less challenging items off your to-do list? Does your ambition to be influential or recognized for your expertise cause you to attend meetings or discussions that don't truly require your involvement? Do you pride yourself on being always ready to answer questions and pitch in on group work? Do you agree to take on collaborative activities because you're worried about being labeled a poor performer or not a team player? Are you uncomfortable staying away from certain issues or projects because you fear missing out on something or aren't sure the work will be done right without you? Most executives we've encountered answer yes to one if not several of those questions.

Efficient collaborators remember that saying yes to something always means saying no to—or participating less fully in—something else. They remind themselves that small wins (an empty inbox, a perfectly worded report, a single client call) are not always important ones. They think carefully about their areas of expertise and determine when they do, or don't, have value to add. They stop seeing themselves as indispensable and shift the source of their self-worth so that it comes from not just showcasing their own capabilities but also stepping away to let others develop theirs and gain visibility.

As one executive told us, "I have come to the realization that if people really need me, they will find me. I am probably skipping 30% of my meetings now, and work seems to be getting done just fine."

When Mike found himself at a breaking point with his twin projects, he realized how much of his self-worth derived from always saying yes to—and then achieving— the goals suggested to him. "It took falling down and a patient spouse to really see this pattern," he says. He decided that he needed to set clear priorities in both his career and his personal life. "Then saying no was not about my not coming through but about maintaining focus on what mattered."

Ellen, too, realized that her self-image as a helper— constantly looking for opportunities to contribute and never declining a request—had become problematic. "The difficult part is recognizing this tendency in the moment and working hard not to jump in," she acknowledges. "But I told my team how important this was and also asked a few people to be 'truth tellers' who caution me when they see it happening."

Eliminating the Unnecessary

Next you'll need to restructure your role, schedule, and network to avoid the triggers you've identified and reduce or eliminate unnecessary collaboration. Rather than thinking things will get better on their own, living reactively, and falling into patterns dictated by other people's objectives, efficient collaborators play offense on collaborative overload. They clarify their "north star" objectives—the strengths they want to employ in their work and the values they want to embody, in the context of their organization's priorities—and then streamline their working lives in a way that buffers them against nonaligned requests.

Start by reviewing your calendar and email communications on a regular basis, using a tool such as Microsoft's MyAnalytics or Cisco's "human network intelligence" platform. Look back four or five months to identify recurring group activities, meetings, or exchanges that aren't core to your success and could be declined or offered to others as a developmental opportunity. Consider decisions you're being pulled into unnecessarily and how processes or teams might be changed so that you needn't be involved. Recognize when you're being sought out for information or expertise in areas no longer central to your role or ambitions and figure out whether you could share your knowledge more widely on your company's intranet or if another go-to person might derive greater benefit from that collaboration.

At the same time, work to reset colleagues' expectations about the level and timeliness of your engagement. Clarify, for example, that not responding to a group email or opting out of a meeting does not mean you lack interest or appreciation. Talk about your key priorities so that everyone knows what you need (and want) to spend the most time on. Ask colleagues about their interests and ambitions so that you can identify opportunities to distribute or delegate work. A key inflection point for all the executives we've counseled has been when they start seeing requests for collaboration as ways to activate and engage those in their networks rather than as adding to their own to-do lists.

Finally, block out time for reflective work and seek collaboration with those who can help you move toward your north star objectives. Mike focused on building capabilities in the business unit he directed. Instead of jumping at unrelated projects for political exposure, he began to differentiate himself through expertise and his team's contribution. Ellen's strategy was to create exceptionally clear boundaries: "I am there 8 a.m. to 6 p.m., and people know I give 100% then. But after that I don't let myself get drawn into unnecessary email, calls, or late-night work just to help out."

Another leader described the shift like this: "Playing defense sucks. You are always reactive and living in fear. The only way to escape it is to get clarity on who you are and what you want to do and start forging a path and network that enable you to get there."

Keeping It Productive

Once you've taken stock of your collaborative workload, it's time to enhance the value of the collaboration you've chosen to participate in. Our research suggests that poorly run meetings are the biggest time sink in organizations. Even if you don't control the ones you attend, you can make them more productive by, for example, asking the leader to circulate an agenda or a pre-read before the gathering and a short email on agreements, commitments, and next steps afterward. You can also limit your involvement by explaining that you have a hard stop (real or constructed) so that you're not stuck when others run overtime, and asking to attend only those portions for which you are needed or agreeing to half the time a colleague or employee requests. It's crucial to establish norms early on in any relationship or group. If you wait, problems will become harder to address.

You can also institute or encourage new norms for emails by addressing format (for example, observing a maximum length and choosing an outline structure with bullets, as opposed to full-text paragraphs), the use of "cc" and "reply all," and appropriate response times for various types of requests. Consider virtual collaboration tools (such as Google Docs), which offer a better medium for work that is exploratory (defining a problem space or brainstorming solutions) or integrative (when people with varying expertise, perspectives, or work assignments need to produce a joint solution). The key is to ensure that you're using the right tools at the right time and not worsening collaborative demands. You should also learn to recognize when a conversation has become too complicated or contentious for email or chat and switch to a more efficient phone call or face-to-face meeting.

For one-on-one interactions, always consider whether you are consuming your counterpart's time efficiently. Ask yourself, "Am I clear on what I want to accomplish from a meeting or a conversation?" And invite others to be equally disciplined by asking early on, "So that I use your time well, would you quickly let me know what you hope we can accomplish together?"

When it comes to building your network, focus on the quality of the relationships, not the number of connections. We repeatedly found that efficient collaborators draw people to collaborative work by conferring status, envisioning joint success, diffusing ownership, and generating a sense of purpose and energy around an outcome. By creating "pull"—rather than simply pushing their agenda—they get greater and more-aligned participation and build trust so that people don't feel the need to seek excessive input or approval.

Ellen, for example, decided to engage stakeholders in collaborative work early to save time later in the process. "I used to dot every i and cross every t before approaching others," she says. "But I've learned that if I get a plan partially developed and then bring in my team, my boss, even my clients, they get invested and help me spot flaws, and I avoid tons of downstream work to fix things or convince people." Another leader we know schedules one-on-ones with direct reports to discuss priorities, values, and personal aspirations, enhancing their ability to work together efficiently as a team in the future. "There are so many ways people can misinterpret actions and then cause a lot of churn later," he says. "If I spend the time to give them a sense of where I'm coming from, it saves all sorts of time in unnecessary collaborations."

The recent explosion in the volume and diversity of collaborative demands is a reality that's here to stay. Unfortunately, the invisible nature of these demands means that few organizations are managing collaborative activity strategically. So it falls to you, the individual, to fight overload and reclaim your collaborative time.

———————————

Rob Cross is the Edward A. Madden Professor of Global Leadership at Babson College and a cofounder and research director of the Connected Commons, a consortium dedicated to helping organizations and individuals thrive in a connected economy.

Scott Taylor is an associate professor of organizational behavior at Babson College.

Deb Zehner is the director of applied research for the Connected Commons.

SECTION TWO

Building the Team

CHAPTER 4

Great Teams Are About Personalities, Not Just Skills

by Dave Winsborough and Tomas Chamorro-Premuzic

At the start of 2016, Google announced that it had discovered the secret ingredients for the perfect team.[1] After years of analyzing interviews and data from more than 100 teams, it found that the drivers of effective team performance are the group's average level of emotional intelligence and a high degree of communication between

Adapted from content posted on hbr.org, January 25, 2017 (product #H03F24).

members. Google's recipe of *being nice* and *joining in* makes perfect sense (and is hardly counterintuitive).

Perhaps more surprising, Google's research implies that the *kinds* of people in the team are not so relevant. While that may be true at Google, a company where people are preselected on the basis of their personality (or "Googliness"), this finding is inconsistent with the wider scientific evidence, which indicates quite clearly that individuals' personalities play a significant role in determining team performance.[2] In particular, personality affects:

- What *role* you have within the team

- How you *interact* with the rest of the team

- Whether your *values* (core beliefs) align with the team's

Importantly, the above processes concern the psychological factors (rather than the technical skills) underlying both individual and team performance. These psychological factors are the main determinants of whether people work together well. If team fit were only about skills and experience, a president might invite political rivals to serve in his administration—yet they may be unlikely to work well together. Likewise, there are often substantial compatibility differences between you and your colleagues, regardless of how similar your expertise and technical backgrounds are.

For example, a study of 133 factory teams found that higher levels of interpersonal sensitivity, curiosity, and emotional stability resulted in more-cohesive teams and increased prosocial behavior among team members.[3] More-effective teams were composed of a higher number of cool-headed, inquisitive, and altruistic people. Along the same lines, a large meta-analysis showed that team members' personalities influence cooperation, shared cognition, information sharing, and overall team performance.[4] In other words, who you are affects how you behave and how you interact with other people, so team members' personalities operate like the different functions of a single organism.

Consider the crew that will one day (soon?) travel to Mars, perhaps working for Elon Musk or one of the government space agencies. Simulations of such voyages put astronauts in cramped quarters for hundreds of days[5] They show that different cliques form in the crew based on values similarity and that higher agreeableness and lower narcissism predict better team cohesion and cooperation.[6]

A useful way to think about teams with the right mix of skills and personalities is to consider the two roles every person plays in a working group: a *functional* role, based on their formal position and technical skill, and a *psychological* role, based on the kind of person they are. Too often, organizations focus merely on the functional role and hope that good team performance somehow follows. This is why even the most expensive professional sports teams often fail to perform according to the individual talents of each player: There is no psychological synergy. A more effective approach (like the mission to

Mars example) focuses as much on people's personalities as on their skills.

In our own work, we found that psychological team roles are largely a product of people's personalities. For example, consider team members who are:

- **Results-oriented.** Team members who naturally organize work and take charge tend to be socially self-confident, competitive, and energetic.

- **Relationship-focused.** Team members who naturally focus on relationships, are attuned to others' feelings, and are good at building cohesion tend to be warm, diplomatic, and approachable.

- **Process and rule followers.** Team members who pay attention to details, processes, and rules tend to be reliable, organized, and conscientious.

- **Innovative and disruptive thinkers.** Team members who naturally focus on innovation, anticipate problems, and recognize when the team needs to change tend to be imaginative, curious, and open to new experiences.

- **Pragmatic.** Team members who are practical, hard-headed challengers of ideas and theories tend to be prudent, emotionally stable, and level-headed.

Observing the balance of roles in a team offers an extraordinary insight into its dynamics. It also indicates the likelihood of success or failure for an assigned task.

For instance, we worked with a finance team charged with rolling out a novel business reporting product for transforming the culture of a staid government agency. But the percentage of players in each role showed the team was doomed from its inception:

- 17% of team members were considered results-oriented.

- 0% of team members were considered good relationship builders.

- 50% of team members were considered process-oriented.

- 0% of team members were considered innovative.

- 100% of team members were considered pragmatic.

Since no one played the relationship-building role, the team lacked internal cohesion and failed to establish any connection with the front-line leaders who were required to take on the team's new accounting process. Similarly, with only a few playing a results-oriented role (and a leader who wasn't one of them), the team struggled to drive itself forward.

Conversely, when too many people play the relationship-building role, it can produce a nice, almost saccharine environment, with too little challenge or contention, as in the leadership team of this social work organization:

- 0% of team members were considered results-oriented.

- 86% of team members were considered good relationship builders.

- 29% of team members were considered process-oriented.

- 29% of team members were considered innovative.

- 0% of team members were considered pragmatic.

In this example, the team spent too much time ensuring harmony and cohesion and too little achieving results. When you focus too much on getting along (with your teammates), you probably will not have much time or energy left for getting ahead (of other teams or organizations).

It is informative to use these kinds of profiles to assess how an incoming team member will impact team performance and dynamics. As the renowned teams researcher Suzanne Bell, who is working on the Mars project for NASA, put it: "We assume that astronauts are intelligent, that they're experts in their technical areas, and that they have at least some teamwork skills. What's tricky is how well individuals combine."[7]

Thus, evaluating the whole person can offer pivotal insights into how people are likely to work together, and can help flag areas of conflict and affinity. Anything of value happens as the result of team effort, where people set aside their selfish interests to achieve something collectively that they could not achieve by themselves. The most successful teams get this mix of personalities right.

Dave Winsborough founded New Zealand's largest psychology practice, Winsborough, and is one of the founders of Deeper Signals, a New York–based firm revolutionizing self-awareness. Previously he was vice president of innovation for Hogan Assessment Systems. Dave is the author of two books and numerous scientific publications. He consults internationally from his base in New Zealand.

Tomas Chamorro-Premuzic is the chief talent scientist at ManpowerGroup, a professor of business psychology at University College London and at Columbia University, and an associate at Harvard's Entrepreneurial Finance Lab. He is the author of *Why Do So Many Incompetent Men Become Leaders? (and How to Fix It)* (Harvard Business Review Press, 2019), upon which his TEDx talk was based. Follow him on Twitter @drtcp.

NOTES

1. Charles Duhigg, "What Google Learned from Its Quest to Build the Perfect Team," *New York Times*, February 25, 2016.

2. Robert P. Tett and Dawn D. Burnett, "A Personality Trait-Based Interactionist Model of Job Performance," *Journal of Applied Psychology* 88, no. 3 (2003): 500–517.

3. Hsiao-Yun Liang et al., "Team Diversity and Team Helping Behavior," *European Management Journal* 33, no. 1 (2015): 48–59.

4. Suzanne Bell et al., "Team Composition and the ABCs of Teamwork," *American Psychologist* 73 (2018): 349-362, https://doi.org/10.1037/amp0000305.

5. G. M. Sandel et al., "Personal Values and Crew Compatibility," *Acta Astronautica* 69 (2011): 141–149.

6. R. M. Rose et al., "Psychological Predictors of Astronaut Effectiveness," *Aviation Space and Environmental Effectiveness* 65 (1994): 910–915.

7. "Mission to Mars," DePaul University, accessed March 4, 2021, https://www.depaul.edu/distinctions/Pages/mission-to-mars.aspx.

CHAPTER 5

Six Ways to Convince Someone to Collaborate with You

by Dorie Clark

Collaboration with the right partner can be the key to unlocking results that neither of you could attain on your own. But it can be challenging to convince someone to collaborate with you, especially if you don't know them well, if there's a (real or perceived) power differential in

Adapted from content posted on hbr.org, December 15, 2020 (product #H061TP).

your relationship, or if you're nervous about asking for help. So what does it take to convince a reluctant potential partner?

If they're a friend or someone who owes you a favor, you might be able to leverage your existing relationship to cajole them into helping you out. Of course, that doesn't mean pressuring them with a mafia-style "offer they can't refuse"—but the personal connection and social norms around reciprocity mean that as long as you ask for their help clearly and directly, they are likely to be fairly open to working with you.

But if you don't already have a strong, preexisting relationship, you'll have to rely on a rational demonstration that a partnership would be mutually beneficial. That means carefully considering their perspective and highlighting exactly what you have to offer them. For instance, if you're looking to convince a celebrity to speak to an academic class you teach, you might not have the budget for a speaking fee—but the engagement could be presented to them as a chance to be viewed more seriously, which they might also find valuable.

Through my experience advising clients and collaborating on various consulting engagements, articles, and even Broadway investments, I've found that there are six types of "collaboration capital" that can help you convince someone to collaborate with you. If you can offer one (or ideally several) of the following forms of capital—and clearly articulate how it will help you and your colleague reach your shared goal—you'll be far more likely to get them on board.

1. Sweat equity

Here's an almost universal law: If you're the one suggesting the partnership, you'll likely need to do most of the work. Especially if your prospective partner has more power or status than you, the extra work is likely a fair trade—after all, the collaboration will likely afford you opportunities that you never would have had access to on your own, no matter how hard you might have been willing to work. Plus, since you're the one who initiated the project, you're probably more motivated about making it happen. Be prepared to write the entire book (and have them weigh in with edits), set up all the meetings and logistics (and have them parachute in at the end to seal the deal), and the like.

2. Subject-matter knowledge

If you've done in-depth research or have deep subject-matter expertise, that can make your proposed collaboration particularly enticing. For example, I'm often approached about collaborating on articles—but I took note when my now-frequent collaborator, David Lancefield, reached out to me last year. He explained that he had conducted a unique and exhaustive survey of how startups are bringing AI to the field of executive coaching, and that he was interested in working together on turning that research into an article. Given my strong interest in the topic, the offer was appealing—I could bring my expertise around synthesizing and presenting data effectively for a business audience, while David's research provided valuable insight that I wouldn't have had access to on my own. I agreed to his offer, and we ended up developing a *Harvard Business Review* article along with another colleague, Dan Cable.

3. Process knowledge

You can often make yourself invaluable if you understand a process that someone else—even someone very accomplished—has no idea how to do. A classic example might be a junior executive showing his boss how to post on Instagram, TikTok, or other social channels. Earlier this year, my colleague Alisa Cohn shared a great idea with me: She wanted to start an online membership community for executive coaches and consultants, focused on the business of coaching and how to drive revenue. She had the subject-matter knowledge to launch the project solo, but she didn't have experience with building online communities, and so she felt unsure about setting up the back end (website, sales mechanisms, etc.). Since I've spent years focused on creating online courses, I suggested a partnership, to which she readily agreed, and we'll be launching next year.

4. Connections

If you're a CEO or a bestselling author, you're likely to have a robust network at your disposal, but there are plenty of occasions when anyone's network can become uniquely valuable. For example, if you're a millennial and your company becomes interested in marketing to the "millennial moms" demographic, your connections could become critical to filling their focus groups and testing new messaging, giving you a potential opportunity to collaborate with senior executives who might otherwise be out of reach. Similarly, if you used to work at a company that your new firm wants to pitch to, your knowledge of their culture and politics could make you a highly valued internal collaborator.

5. Access to funding

Financing can take many forms. Producers often land the opportunity to work with prominent playwrights or directors because they agree to put up the money for their next show. Similarly, angel investors or VCs often get to collaborate with successful startup founders when they fund their companies. But direct access to cash isn't the only way you can leverage funding to convince a potential partner to work with you. A variation that's more accessible for many professionals is simply to have a deal "in the bag" before approaching a potential collaborator. For many projects, the hard part is landing the business, so if you already have a deal arranged with clear terms (that is, "IBM will pay us X amount per workshop, and you'll get Y percent of that"), it's surprisingly easy to get a yes.

To give you a sense for what not to do, I once had a colleague propose that I fly to her state to conduct an open-enrollment workshop with her, without any discernable business pipeline or marketing plan to fill the seats. The event itself might have been interesting, but it seemed more like wishful thinking than an actual proposal, and so I declined—whereas if she'd had a corporate client already on board, I likely would have agreed.

6. Image

How a person is perceived is often the very reason you're approaching them for a collaboration: If they're well known and respected, you might try to collaborate with them in the hopes that their stature will help your project succeed. But this can actually go both ways. Even if you're the junior partner in the equation, you might have more to offer than you realize when it comes to burnishing a potential collaborator's image.

In many cases, while the collaboration may enable the junior colleague to tap into a measure of gravitas, the senior colleague stands to gain recognition among a new audience and a share of "hipness"—think collaborations between older musicians and the "next generation," such as that of Tony Bennett and Lady Gaga back in 2014. Similarly, if you've established yourself in a cutting-edge area (such as social media, AI, emerging international markets, or anything seen as a growth area in your company), that may make you a more appealing partner to even a senior-level colleague.

When done right, collaboration is a powerful tool—a merging of your unique talents and those of your partner to achieve valuable results. But too often, even smart professionals fail to grasp their own value, and thus don't articulate a sufficiently compelling proposition to their would-be partners. By understanding the "collaboration capital" you bring—and communicating it with confidence, without veering into arrogance—you're far more likely to win over your colleague and be on your way to accomplishing great things together.

———————

Dorie Clark is a marketing strategist and professional speaker who teaches at Duke University's Fuqua School of Business. She is the author of *Entrepreneurial You* (Harvard Business Review Press, 2017), *Reinventing You* (Harvard Business Review Press, 2017), and *Stand Out*. You can receive her free Recognized Expert self-assessment at www.dorieclark.com/hbrtoolkit.

CHAPTER 6

Making Star Teams Out of Star Players

by Michael Mankins, Alan Bird, and James Root

When it comes to an organization's scarcest resource—talent—the difference between the best and the rest is enormous. In fields that involve repetitive, transactional tasks, top performers are typically two or three times as productive as others. Justo Thomas, the best fish butcher at Le Bernardin restaurant in New York, can portion as much fish in an hour as the average prep cook can manage in three hours. In highly specialized or creative work, the differential is likely to be a factor of six or more.

Adapted from an article in *Harvard Business Review*, January-February 2013 (product #R1301E).

Before becoming chief justice of the U.S. Supreme Court, John Roberts prevailed in 25 of the 39 cases he argued before the Court. That record is almost nine times better than the average record of other winning attorneys (excluding solicitors general) who have argued before the Court since 1950. Across all job types, we estimate, the best performers are roughly four times as productive as average performers. That holds in every industry, geographical region, and type of organization we've examined.

Why, then, do companies so rarely bring together a team of star players to tackle a big challenge? The easy answer—indeed, the conventional wisdom—is that all-star teams just don't work. Egos will take over. The stars won't work well with one another. They'll drive the team leader crazy.

We think it's time to reconsider that assumption. To be sure, managing a team of stars is not for the faint of heart. (The conventional wisdom is there for a reason.) But when the stakes are high—when a business model needs to be reinvented, say, or a key new product designed, or a strategic problem solved—doesn't it seem foolish not to put your best people on the job, provided you can find a way to manage them effectively?

We have seen all-star teams do extraordinary work. For example, it took just 600 Apple engineers less than two years to develop, debug, and deploy OS X, a revolutionary change in the company's operating system. By contrast, it took as many as 10,000 engineers more than five years to develop, debug, deploy, and eventually retract Microsoft's Windows Vista.

Common sense suggests that all-star teams would have two big advantages.

Sheer firepower

If you have world-class talent of all kinds on a team, you multiply the productivity and performance advantages that stand-alone stars deliver. Consider auto-racing pit crews. Kyle Busch's six-man crew is widely considered the finest on the NASCAR circuit. And each member is the best for his position—gas man, jackman, tire carriers, and tire changers. Crew members train together year-round with one clear goal in mind: to get Busch's #18 racer in and out of the pit in the shortest possible time. The crew can execute a standard pit stop—73 maneuvers, including refueling and a change of all four tires—in 12.12 seconds. Add just one average player to Busch's crew—say, an ordinary tire changer—and that time nearly doubles, to 23.09 seconds. Add two average team members to the mix, and it climbs to well over half a minute.

Synergy

Putting the best thinkers together can spur creativity and ideas that no one member of the team would have developed alone. The blockbuster movie *Toy Story*—the top-grossing film of 1995—wasn't the product of one visionary filmmaker. Rather, it was the result of an often prickly but ultimately productive collaboration among Pixar's top artists and animators, Disney's veteran executives (including Jeffrey Katzenberg, then head of the film division), and Steve Jobs. The Pixar team originally presented Disney with what Katzenberg deemed an un-inspiring tale. A major revision—far more edgy, at Katzenberg's insistence—lacked the cheeriness essential to a family movie. Finally the all-star group came up with something that satisfied everyone on the team—and that would later be dubbed by *Time* magazine "the year's most inventive comedy."

To do their best, alpha teams need leaders and support staff who are all-stars too. Extremely talented people have often never worked for someone they can learn a lot from; in our experience, most relish the opportunity and pull out all the stops. And high-caliber subordinates allow team members to accomplish more. A gifted administrative assistant, for example, requires less direction and competently shoulders many routine tasks, so the other team members can focus on what they do best.

Let's look at what else you need to have in place before you even think about putting together a star team. We'll also examine what kinds of work these teams are best suited for and how to manage the very real difficulties they may present.

The Table Stakes: Good Talent Management

A surprising number of companies don't follow basic best practices for talent management. Without these in place, there's no hope of making all-star teams effective.

Understand where your strengths are

Companies that are good at managing "A" players keep comprehensive, granular data on where their people are currently deployed, what those people do, how good they are in their current roles, and how transferable their skills may be. The companies use that information to continually improve their staffing resources and deploy them more effectively. Take AllianceBernstein (AB), a $3 billion asset management company based in Manhattan and a leading equity research firm. The firm carefully rates each of its 3,700 employees every year along two dimensions: performance and potential. The senior team at AB spends several days together each year cross-calibrating both sets of ratings across the entire company.

It's also critical to understand employees' ability to fill roles outside their current one. When Caesars Entertainment, the gaming company, reorganized operations in 2011, the senior team not only developed a database on the performance and potential of the company's top 2,000 managers but also analyzed the ability of the top 150 to take on new and different jobs.

Finally, watch out for talent hoarding. In too many organizations, star players are confined to a division, hidden from the leaders of other divisions. But no company can deploy talent effectively if it doesn't treat its best people like a shared asset rather than the property of a particular unit.

Don't create disincentives for teamwork

Some companies' performance assessment methods get in the way of team success. Microsoft is an example. For many years the software giant used a "stack ranking" system as part of its performance evaluation model.

At regular intervals, a certain percentage of any team's members would be rated "top performers," "good," "average," "below average," and "poor," regardless of the team's overall performance. In some situations this kind of forced ranking is effective, but in Microsoft's case it had unintended consequences. Over time, according to insiders' reports, the stack ranking created a culture in which employees competed with one another rather than against other companies. "A" players rarely liked to join groups with other "A" players, because they feared they might be seen as the weakest members of the team.

Own the pipeline

When big strategic goals are involved, a company often finds that it needs capabilities it doesn't have. The wise leader anticipates this problem by actively and continually looking for talent. The individuals responsible for executing strategy must have an ownership stake in this recruiting process, because talent is always a key component of strategy. Yet many companies continue to subcontract recruiting wholesale to the HR department and professional search firms.

Play Your Best Hand: Choose Mission-Critical Projects

We don't recommend putting together an alpha team for small projects. They're not worth the trouble or the opportunity costs. Save such teams for initiatives that have clearly defined objectives and are critical to the company's strategy. Product development efforts often fit this category, and others may as well.

Boeing's 777 airliner provides a good example of what a star team can achieve in product development. Back in 1990, Boeing recognized that it had an important gap in its offerings: It had no airplane positioned between its jumbo 747 jetliner and its midsize 767 model. To address this gap, Boeing assembled a team of its best engineers.

The design effort was different from anything the company had previously done. To be sure, there were other important factors in its success—direct input from customers, new use of technology—but it took these alpha players to master the project's extreme complexity and bring it together. The basic design was completed in less than four months. The plane entered service in less than five years. By assembling its engineering stars and having them work side by side with customers, the company was able to launch what many industry analysts view as the most successful airplane program in commercial aviation history, with nearly 950 aircraft in service today. Moreover, Boeing got the 777 to market faster than any other major plane before.

Product development projects aren't the only promising opportunities for all-star teams. Sometimes a functional overhaul rises to the level of strategic importance, as it did for Caesars Entertainment, which operates casino properties throughout the world, mainly under the Caesars, Harrah's, and Horseshoe brands. Prior to 2011, Caesars' marketing budget was managed jointly by the company's 42 U.S. properties, with each casino's marketing organization determining what promotions to offer, when to offer them, which customers to target, and so on. The trouble was that marketing performance varied greatly: The success rate for the best properties was nearly four times that of the average property. Starting in 2011, the company assembled a team of six "pod leaders" to direct marketing spending for its properties in the United States. The team, drawn from the company's most experienced marketers and comprising individuals with a wide range of exceptional skills, completely revamped Caesars' promotions. It eliminated overlapping promotions. It tested new promotions at one property before rolling them out systemwide. It focused investments on promotions that had a demonstrated track record of generating profitable revenue. Transforming the company's whole marketing effort in this manner was a difficult, complicated task that might easily have overwhelmed a less skilled team. Yet the results were dramatic: The number of unprofitable promotions across Caesars declined by more than 20%, and the incremental profit generated by the average promotion increased by more than 10%.

Manage the Odds: Anticipate What Could Go Wrong

Even if you have excellent talent management practices in place and you've loosed your all-star team on a well-defined, strategically relevant problem, you may still face challenges. Here's what to watch out for, along with some tips for avoiding problems.

Big egos, little progress

Egos can get in the way of team performance. But they don't have to. In 1992, America's first "Dream Team"—

made up of the very best basketball players in the NBA—swept the Olympic Games in Barcelona, defeating its opponents by an average of 44 points. This team succeeded because the goal of representing the United States with honor at the Olympics was bigger than any one player. It also helped that team performance was the basis for members' rewards: Nobody was going to get an individual medal. These are two points that organizations creating all-star teams should keep in mind. They should also prune anyone who isn't a team player from the group, regardless of how good that person may be.

Overshadowing the rest of the cast

The use of "A" teams can lead to a system in which only the best feel valued, thereby demoralizing average performers. One antidote is to ensure that everyone shares in the "A" team's achievements. George Clooney and the rest of his all-star cast on *Ocean's Eleven* created an environment where cast and crew reveled in their mutual success. Reportedly, most crew members were so pleased with the experience that they sought to sign on for *Ocean's Twelve* and *Ocean's Thirteen*. Other ways to keep "B" players engaged include recognizing performance, whether it's mission-critical or not; using a common performance evaluation system for stars and nonstars; and establishing common rewards shared by all involved.

Great team members, mediocre leaders

All-star teams headed by poor leaders can produce mediocre results. Imagine a chamber orchestra made up of virtuosos—think Itzhak Perlman, Gil Shaham, Yuri Bashmet, Yo-Yo Ma, and their peers—but conducted by an amateur. The 12-instrument arrangement of Stravinsky's Concertino might never recover. To avoid this scenario, an organization should invest as much time in picking team leaders as in picking members, ask members for feedback on the leader early (and often), and not be afraid to switch generals or even to promote a team member to leader. Ask any group of senior executives about which resources they don't have enough of, and they are likely to acknowledge that star talent is one of the scarcest. Then ask them how confident they are that their companies deploy and manage their best players to have the greatest impact on the bottom line, and they will probably express reservations. Is it possible that executives are overlooking one powerful tool that could help them achieve that goal?

Michael Mankins is a partner in Bain & Company's Austin office and a leader in the firm's Organization and Strategy practices. He is a coauthor of *Time, Talent, Energy: Overcome Organizational Drag and Unleash Your Team's Productive Power* (Harvard Business Review Press, 2017).

Alan Bird is an advisory partner and founder of Bain's Results Delivery practice. He is based in London.

James Root is a senior partner in Bain's Consumer Products and Organization practices and chairman of Bain Futures. He is based in Hong Kong.

CHAPTER 7

Ensuring Agile Teams Can Work Together

by Alia Crocker, Rob Cross, and Heidi K. Gardner

Agile collaboration is more critical than ever. Organizations today need to be continually on the lookout for new market developments and competitive threats, identifying relevant experts and nimbly forming and disbanding teams to help tackle those issues quickly. However, these cross-functional groups often bump up against misaligned incentives, hierarchical decision making, and cultural rigidities, causing progress to stall or action to not be taken at all.

Adapted from "How to Make Sure Agile Teams Can Work Together," on hbr.org, May 15, 2018 (product #H04BXH).

Consider the case of an organization in our consortium, the Connected Commons, that uncovered a groundbreaking audio/visual technology that would differentiate the organization in existing channels but also had the potential to open up entirely new markets. The CEO heralded it as a pivot point in growth and formed a cross-functional initiative of 100+ top employees to bring it to new commercial channels. Yet, unfortunately progress did not match expectations. Employees assigned to the effort struggled to make time for the work. They often did not understand the expertise or values of different functions and advocated too aggressively for their own solutions. The group was surprised several times by the demands of external stakeholders. Despite this project's visibility, critical mandate, and groundbreaking technology, the organization was ultimately hindered when it came to agile collaboration. This story is not unique.

A significant part of the problem is that work occurs through collaboration in networks of relationships that often do not mirror formal reporting structures or standard work processes. Intuitively, we know that the collaborative intensity of work has skyrocketed, and that collaborations are central to agility. Yet most organizations don't manage internal collaboration productively and assume that technology or formal org charts can yield agility. These efforts often fail because they lack informal networks—for example, employees who share an interest in a technological innovation like artificial intelligence or a passion for environmental sustainability, who can bridge the organization's entrepreneurial and operational systems by bringing cutting-edge ideas to people who have the resources to begin experimenting and implementing them.

Our research focuses on agility not as a broad ideal, but rather on where it matters most—at the point of execution, where teams are working on new products, strategic initiatives, or with top clients. All of these points of execution are essential for organizations, yet all encounter inefficiencies unless they're managed as a network. We assessed these strategically important groups in a wide range of global organizations via network surveys, which were completed by more than 30,000 employees. We also conducted hundreds of interviews with both workers and leaders in these companies. We found that agility at the point of execution is typically created through group-level networks such as account or new product development teams formed from employees drawn throughout the organization, lateral networks across core work processes, temporary teams and task forces formed to drive a critical organizational change or respond to a strategic threat, and communities of practice that enable organizations to enjoy true benefits of scale. These and other lateral networks provide agility when they are nurtured along four dimensions: (1) managing the center of the network, (2) engaging the fringe, (3) bridging select silos, and (4) leveraging boundary spanners. Leaders who nurture their internal networks in this way produce better outcomes—financial, strategic, and talent-related.[1] (See figure 7-1.)

FIGURE 7-1

To manage collaboration, pay attention to 4 points of execution

Ask yourself if you're identifying networks' centers, leveraging their edges, bringing silos together, and making external connections.

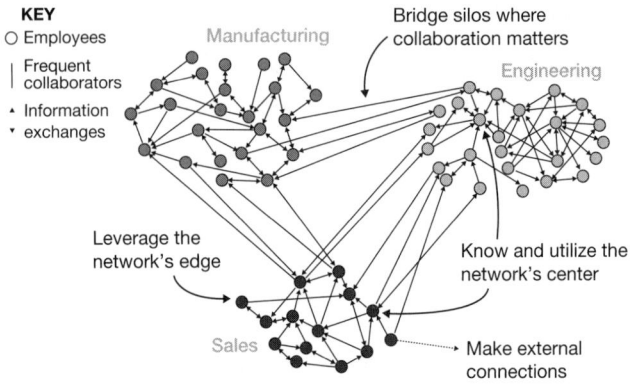

Source: Alia Crocker et al.

Managing the Network's Center

When agility is viewed through a network lens, it becomes apparent that collaboration is never equally distributed. We typically see that 20% to 35% of valuable collaborations come from only 3% to 5% of employees. Through no fault of their own, these people become overly relied upon and tend to slow group responsiveness, despite working to their wits' end.[2] They are more likely to burn out and leave the company, creating network gaps, which then become another barrier to agility. Senior leaders need to consider where overload on the network's center might preclude agile collaboration and:

- **Encourage overwhelmed employees to redistribute collaborative work** in conjunction with their managers. Groundbreaking work from the Institute for Corporate Productivity found that acknowledging and shifting collaborative demands in this way is a practice that's three times more likely to be found in high-performing organizations compared to those with lower performance.

- **Understand how employees have ended up in the center.** And if it is a result of formal position or personal characteristics, then take the corrective actions necessary to reduce overload. For example, simple shifts in a few behaviors can yield as much as 18% to 24% more time for collaboration. Such behaviors include managing meetings more efficiently, creating an effective climate of email use, blocking time in calendars for reflective work, negotiating role demands, and avoiding triggers that lead us all to jump in on projects or meetings when we shouldn't, to name just a few.

- **Map the interdependencies between different teams** where your central players contribute, in order to understand and plan for potential risks. When a star sits at the center of multiple projects, a surprise shock in one team can create nasty ripples well beyond the jolted team. Be sure team leaders have a backup plan to cover these emergencies.

Engaging the Network's Fringe Players

Agility requires the integration of different capabilities and perspectives to understand VUCA issues (volatility, uncertainty, complexity, and ambiguity) and figure out what kinds of experts are needed to tackle them. But those who see the world differently or who are new to a group often languish at the network edges. Whereas those in the center may be overrelied upon, those on the fringes are often not tapped in a way that allows for agile collaboration. For example, our research shows that it can take three to five years for a newcomer to replicate the connectivity of a high performer.[3] Few organizations provide such luxury of time, however: Our research also shows that if an experienced hire doesn't get integrated into substantive projects *within the first year*, they are seriously at risk of leaving before they reach the three-year mark.

Getting others to trust fringe employees is essential for drawing them into agile collaboration. Their competence isn't usually in question, if you have rigorous hiring and merit-based promotion processes; the trick is getting others to trust their motives ("Will he take undue credit?" or "Will she walk away with my clients?") if few colleagues can vouch for their character. Senior management can help by taking the following actions:

- Create a "hidden gems" program to help unearth high-potential but overlooked experts who could take some of the burden off of overworked central players. Role-model this behavior by, for example, assigning an up-and-comer to co-lead a high-status initiative.

- **Help those on the fringe to create "pull" for their work.** Instead of pushing expertise on others across the network, these employees need to be seen as a strategic resource to be pulled into opportunities. This is done by identifying mutual value and matching capabilities from the fringe to needs across the network.

- **Pair newcomers and network influencers through staffing or mentoring.** This simple practice triples newcomer connectivity compared to those who do not get this experience.

- **Create inclusive and trusting environments to facilitate agile collaboration.** A culture of fear exists when employees do not feel safe to come forward with ideas, and those on the fringe may be less confident about contributing. High-performing organizations are 2.5 times more likely to facilitate an environment of safe communication.[4]

Bridging Select Silos

Every organization we studied struggled with silos across functions, expertise, geography, level, and cultures—whether occupational or national. The network lens can help uncover specific points that if crossed could yield agility benefits, rather than inefficiently bridging all silos. Often, this means connecting people across units or geographies doing similar work to yield benefits of scale, or identifying points where integrating different perspectives yields agile innovation. This type of multidisciplinary collaboration produces higher revenues and profits because it tackles higher-value problems.[5] Motivating experts to engage in agile collaboration requires them not only to identify and appreciate knowledge from other silos, but also to be willing to give up some control and autonomy over a project's direction. Senior leaders can help motivate experts with the following actions:

- **Set specific goals and reward agile collaboration.** Our research found that, compared to lower performing organizations, high-performance organizations are three to five times more likely to reward collaboration, motivating employees to move beyond silos.[6] Our studies of firms that use peer feedback to effectively identify and celebrate agile collaborators show that these bottom-up processes often uncover excellent people whom the formal performance reviews might otherwise overlook.

- **Use data and analytics to understand where silos exist, in order to unlock possible agile collaboration.** In one study, we found discrepancies in connections between headquarters and affiliates, and poor collaboration between engineering and sales. This insight produced the business case for holding brainstorming sessions to build connections and improve communication. A data-driven approach not only is more accurate and less biased than relying on individuals' perceptions, but also more convincingly demonstrates the quantifiable upside for agile collaboration.

- **Identify experts scattered across silos and key cross-points in the firm for agile collaboration.** Set up communities of practice or business development initiatives to help share expertise or resources. For example, many business service firms are prompting professionals who serve customers in similar industries such as insurance or biotech to meet informally and share sector insights and leads. Those who are well connected act as bridges to and from silos. Some firms have successfully tasked high-potential employees with tracking the evolving expertise in adjacent departments, which has to be a dynamic process, definitely not a knowledge database. These employees should be recognized for identifying opportunities to use cross-silo knowledge. Exchange programs or rotational programs can help here, too.

Spanning External Boundaries

Agility thrives when employees understand their organization within the broader ecosystem, and continually scan for market developments that pose either threats or opportunities. Doing so requires dynamic knowledge of external bodies such as competitors, customers, regulators, and expertise communities or associations. Those who span the boundary between internal and external actors can solve problems in unique ways, because they can access knowledge from these different worlds. They can also facilitate agile collaboration by efficiently integrating disparate viewpoints and creating multistakeholder solutions, but they need to be properly empowered, managed, and resourced in order to do so. Senior managers can facilitate this by doing the following:

- **Identify and enlist boundary spanners to help tackle vexing problems.** People who connect the organization with its ecosystem can propose plans that can be feasibly implemented, since they have access to the shortest informational paths in the network and legitimacy in the broader environmental context.

- **Nurture relationships and promote the exchange of information by organizing forums or special events that convene key players from across the ecosystem.** This approach helps to create more people in your organization who are capable of functioning as bridges to external parties, and it provides insights on pain points and opportunities in the ecosystem.

- **Promote connectivity to key external stakeholders.** High-performing organizations are 2.5 times more likely to encourage interaction with external stakeholders such as clients, suppliers, regulatory bodies, or professional associations.[7] Senior managers should require employees who are well connected internally to work on external connections or suggest that those who are well connected externally mentor junior employees in networking to ensure boundary spanning.

Managing these collaborative players as part of a network can help organizations be more agile. Although agile collaboration requires continual reassessment of complex problems, it is possible for firms to combine and recombine essential expertise from across points in the network to address VUCA issues. By steadily nurturing agile collaboration, senior management can more effectively and more efficiently access the necessary depth of expertise of key collaborators within the organization.

Alia Crocker is an assistant professor of strategy at Babson College and focuses on issues related to strategic human capital in her research, teaching, and consulting work.

Rob Cross is the Edward A. Madden Professor of Global Leadership at Babson College and a cofounder and research director of the Connected Commons, a consortium dedicated to helping organizations and individuals thrive in a connected economy.

Heidi K. Gardner is a distinguished fellow at Harvard Law School and a faculty chair in the school's executive education programs. She is also a cofounder of Gardner & Co.

NOTES

1. Heidi K. Gardner, "When Senior Managers Won't Collaborate," *Harvard Business Review*, March 2015.

2. Rob Cross et al., "Collaborative Overload," *Harvard Business Review*, January 2016.

3. "Connect and Adapt," Connected Commons, video, n.d., http://www.connectedcommons.com/connect-adapt-improving-retention-engagement-first-five-years-video.

4. "Purposeful Collaboration," Institute for Corporate Productivity, 2017, http://go.i4cp.com/purposefulcollaboration.pdf.

5. Gardner, "When Senior Managers Won't Collaborate."

6. "Purposeful Collaboration," Institute for Corporate Productivity.

7. "Purposeful Collaboration," Institute for Corporate Productivity.

Being Productive as a Team

CHAPTER 8

High-Performing Teams Need Psychological Safety

by Laura Delizonna

"There's no team without trust," says Paul Santagata, head of industry at Google. He knows the results of the tech giant's massive two-year study on team performance, which revealed that the highest-performing teams have one thing in common: psychological safety, the belief that you won't be punished when you make a

---

Adapted from "High-Performing Teams Need Psychological Safety. Here's How to Create It," on hbr.org, August 24, 2017 (product #H03TK7).

mistake.[1] Studies show that psychological safety allows for moderate risk taking, speaking your mind, creativity, and sticking your neck out without fear of having it cut off—just the types of behavior that lead to market breakthroughs.[2]

Ancient evolutionary adaptations explain why psychological safety is both fragile and vital to success in uncertain, interdependent environments. The brain processes a provocation by a boss, competitive coworker, or dismissive subordinate as a life-or-death threat. The amygdala, the alarm bell in the brain, ignites the fight-or-flight response, hijacking higher brain centers. This "act first, think later" brain structure shuts down perspective and analytical reasoning. Quite literally, just when we need it most, we lose our minds. While that fight-or-flight reaction may save us in life-or-death situations, it handicaps the strategic thinking needed in today's workplace.

Twenty-first-century success depends on another system—the broaden-and-build mode of positive emotion, which allows us to solve complex problems and foster cooperative relationships. Barbara Fredrickson at the University of North Carolina has found that positive emotions like trust, curiosity, confidence, and inspiration broaden the mind and help us build psychological, social, and physical resources.[3] We become more open-minded, resilient, motivated, and persistent when we feel safe. Humor increases, as does solution finding and divergent thinking—the cognitive process underlying creativity.

When the workplace feels challenging but not threatening, teams can sustain the broaden-and-build mode. Oxytocin levels in our brains rise, eliciting trust and trust-making behavior. This is a huge factor in team success, as Santagata attests: "In Google's fast-paced, highly demanding environment, our success hinges on the ability to take risks and be vulnerable in front of peers."

So how can you increase psychological safety on your own team? Try replicating the steps that Santagata took:

1. Approach conflict as a collaborator, not an adversary

We humans hate losing even more than we love winning, according to the prospect theory of psychology. A perceived loss triggers attempts to reestablish fairness through competition, criticism, or disengagement, which is a form of workplace-learned helplessness. Santagata knows that true success is a win-win outcome, so when conflicts come up, he avoids triggering a fight-or-flight reaction by asking, "How could we achieve a mutually desirable outcome?"

2. Speak human to human

Underlying every team's who-did-what confrontation are universal needs such as respect, competence, social status, and autonomy. Recognizing these deeper needs naturally elicits trust and promotes positive language and behaviors. Santagata reminded his team that even in the most contentious negotiations, the other party is just like them and aims to walk away happy. He led them through a reflection called "Just Like Me," which asks you to consider:

- This person has beliefs, perspectives, and opinions, just like me.

- This person has hopes, anxieties, and vulnerabilities, just like me.

- This person has friends, family, and perhaps children who love them, just like me.

- This person wants to feel respected, appreciated, and competent, just like me.

- This person wishes for peace, joy, and happiness, just like me.

3. Anticipate reactions and plan countermoves

"Thinking through in advance how your audience will react to your messaging helps ensure your content will be heard, versus your audience hearing an attack on their identity or ego," explains Santagata.

Skillfully confront difficult conversations head-on by preparing for likely reactions. For example, you may need to gather concrete evidence to counter defensiveness when discussing hot-button issues. Santagata asks himself, "If I position my point in this manner, what are the possible objections, and how would I respond to those counterarguments?" He says, "Looking at the discussion from this third-party perspective exposes weaknesses in my positions and encourages me to rethink my argument."

Specifically, he asks:

- What are my main points?

- What are three ways my listeners are likely to respond?

- How will I respond to each of those scenarios?

4. Replace blame with curiosity

If team members sense that you're trying to blame them for something, you become their saber-toothed tiger. John Gottman's research at the University of Washington shows that blame and criticism reliably escalate conflict, leading to defensiveness and—eventually—to disengagement. The alternative to blame is curiosity. If you believe you already know what the other person is thinking, then you're not ready to have a conversation. Instead, adopt a learning mindset, knowing you don't have all the facts. Here's how:

- State the problematic behavior or outcome as an observation, and use factual, neutral language. For example, "In the past two months there's been a noticeable drop in your participation during meetings and progress appears to be slowing on your project."

- Engage them in an exploration. For example, "I imagine there are multiple factors at play. Perhaps we could uncover what they are together?"

- Ask for solutions. The people who are responsible for creating a problem often hold the keys to solving it. That's why a positive outcome typically depends on their input and buy-in. Ask directly, "What do you think needs to happen here?" Or, "What would be your ideal scenario?" Another question leading to solutions is: "How could I support you?"

5. Ask for feedback on delivery

Asking for feedback on how you delivered your message disarms your opponent, illuminates blind spots in communication skills, and models fallibility, which increases trust in leaders.[4] Santagata closes difficult conversations with these questions:

- What worked and what didn't work in my delivery?

- How did it feel to hear this message?

- How could I have presented it more effectively?

For example, Santagata asked about his delivery after giving his senior manager tough feedback. His manager replied, "This could have felt like a punch in the stomach, but you presented reasonable evidence and that made me want to hear more. You were also eager to discuss the challenges I had, which led to solutions."

6. Measure psychological safety

Santagata periodically asks his team how safe they feel and what could enhance their feeling of safety. In addition, his team routinely takes surveys on psychological safety and other team dynamics. Some teams at Google include questions such as, "How confident are you that you won't receive retaliation or criticism if you admit an error or make a mistake?"

If you create this sense of psychological safety on your own team starting now, you can expect to see higher levels of engagement, increased motivation to tackle difficult problems, more learning and development opportunities, and better performance.

Laura Delizonna, PhD, is an executive coach, instructor at Stanford University, international speaker, and founder of Delizonna.com.

NOTES

1. Julia Rozovsky, "The Five Keys to A Successful Google Team," Re:Work, November 17, 2015, https://rework.withgoogle.com/blog/five-keys-to-a-successful-google-team/.

2. Amy Edmondson, "Psychological Behavior and Learning Behavior in Work Teams," *Administrative Science Quarterly* 44, no. 2 (1999); Steven P. Brown and Thomas W. Leigh, "A New Look at Psychological Climate and and Its Relationship to Job Involvement, Effort, and Performance," *Journal of Applied Psychology* 81, no. 4 (1996): 358–368.

3. Barbara L. Fredrickson, "Positive Emotions Broaden and Build" in *Advances on Experimental Social Psychology, Volume 47*, ed. E. Ashby Plant and Patricia G. Devine (Academic Press, 2013) 1-46. https://peplab.web.unc.edu/wp-content/uploads/sites/18901/2019/06/Fredrickson2013ChapteronBnBinAESP.pdf.

4. Bradley P. Owens et al., "Exploring the Relevance and Implications of Humility in Organizations," *Handbook of Positive Organizational Scholarship*, September 1, 2010.

CHAPTER 9

The Best Teams Have Clearly Defined Roles

by Tammy Erickson

Which is more important to promoting collaboration: a clearly defined approach toward achieving the goal, or clearly specified roles for individual team members? The common assumption—and my personal approach for many years—is that carefully spelling out the approach is essential, while leaving the roles of individuals within the team open and flexible will encourage people to share ideas and contribute on multiple dimensions.

Adapted from "The Biggest Mistake You (Probably) Make with Teams," on hbr.org, April 05, 2012 (product # H008KX).

But our research has shown that the opposite is true: Collaboration improves when the roles of individual team members are clearly defined and well understood—in fact, when individuals feel their role is bounded in ways that allow them to do a significant portion of their work independently. Without such clarity, team members are likely to waste energy negotiating roles or protecting turf, rather than focusing on the task.

We've also found that team members are more likely to want to collaborate if the path to achieving the team's goal is left somewhat ambiguous. If a team perceives the task as one that requires creativity, where the approach is not yet well known or predefined, its members are more likely to invest more time and energy in collaboration.

Consider a team of doctors and nurses working in a hospital emergency room. Before the next ambulance arrives, they have no idea of the nature of the task ahead. Will the patient require surgery, heart resuscitation, medications? The condition of the next patient is unknown; the tasks that will be required of the team, ambiguous. But at no time while the team waits, do they negotiate roles: "Who would like to administer the anesthesia? Who will set out the instruments? Who will make key decisions?" Each role is clear. As a result, when the patient arrives, the team is able to move quickly into action.

At the BBC, we studied the teams responsible for the radio and television broadcasts of special events and daytime television news. These teams were large—ranging from 66 people in one case to 133 in another—and included members with a wide range of skills and from many disciplines. One would imagine, therefore, that there was a high possibility of confusion among team members.

To the contrary, we found that the BBC's teams scored among the highest in our sample with regard to the clarity with which team members viewed their own roles and the roles of others. Every team was composed of specialists who had deep expertise in their given function, and each person had a clearly defined role. There was no overlap in the responsibilities of the sound technician and of the camera operator, and so on. Yet the tasks the BBC teams tackle are, by their very nature, uncertain and to some extent ambiguous, particularly when they involve covering breaking news. The trick the BBC and others in the film industry have pulled off has been to clarify team members' individual roles with so much precision that it keeps friction, internal competition and the possibility of mistakes of omission to a minimum.

In the same research, we also studied successful teams at Reuters—teams that worked out of far-flung locations and, in many cases, didn't speak a common language. (The primary languages were Russian, Chinese, Thai, and English.) These teams, largely composed of software programmers, were responsible for the rapid development of highly complex technical software and network products. Many of the programmers sat at their desks for 12 hours straight developing code, speaking with no one. Each individual was given autonomy for one discrete, well-defined piece of the project; the rapid pace and demanding project timelines encouraged individual members to work independently to get the job done. Yet because each individual's work had to fit seamlessly into the final product, shaped with an eye toward achieving the overall team goal, these teams judged collaborative behavior to be high among their members.

The leader's role, as I learned from this research, is to ensure that the roles and responsibilities of the team members are clearly defined for the specific project at hand (members' roles may change from project to project to provide variety and broaden experience). Conversely, leaders should help team members understand the project's importance and ultimate objective but leave the exact approach to the discretion of the team.

Tamara J. Erickson has authored *Retire Retirement* (2008), *Plugged In* (2008), and *What's Next, Gen X?* (2010), all published by Harvard Business Review Press. She is the author or coauthor of five *Harvard Business Review* articles and the book *Workforce Crisis* (Harvard Business Review Press, 2006). Erickson was named one of the top 50 global business thinkers for 2011.

CHAPTER 10

Helping Teams with Different Subcultures to Collaborate

by Roger Schwarz

The term "organizational culture" can obscure an important truth: An organization often contains many cultures. This is true even if your organization is located entirely in one country, or even at one site.

Because each business unit or team may have their own subculture, working effectively across the organization requires skill in working across cultures.

Adapted from "Getting Teams with Different Subcultures to Collaborate," on hbr.org, July 22, 2016 (product #H030U7).

Doing this requires three steps: understanding what culture is and how it works, identifying the cultures of your team and the teams you work with, and designing how you and the other teams will work together.

Understand what team culture is and how it works

A team's culture is its shared values and assumptions, and it results from a mix of elements: the organization, industry, geographic region and nation, and profession or function the team represents. Values are things we consider worth striving for, such as honesty, account-ability, and compassion. Assumptions are beliefs we hold about how the world works or how things are related. For example, you may assume that people generally want to do a good job, or that people are more committed to a decision when they are involved in making it. A team manifests its culture in many artifacts, including norms that lead members to act in certain ways and to create structures, processes, and policies. It's important to distinguish between a team's espoused culture and the one it operates from. The values that team members *say* they operate from are the espoused culture—which may or may not be what they actually operate from.

Identify your team's and other teams' cultures

To determine how cultures differ, you need to identify the values and assumptions that constitute them. And to do that you need to operate from the assumption that differences are opportunities for learning; if that thinking isn't already part of your culture, your joint exploration may quickly devolve into conflict as each team describes how the other's culture is a problem. To avoid this, consider finding a facilitator or consultant to help you.

Start by identifying artifacts that strike each team as notably different from its own. This includes norms, behaviors, structures, and processes. For example, you may notice that the team you're working with spends significant time trying to agree on what important words mean, while your team considers these detailed conversations to be a poor use of time. Or the other team may point out that your team deals with inter-team conflicts by raising the issue in the full inter-team meeting, while their team discusses conflicts in private.

Next, identify the assumptions and values that generate these artifacts. In the example above, your team raising conflicts in the full group may reflect your belief that conflict can best be resolved in the setting where all the information exists. The other team may assume that conflicts are best resolved in private where people are less likely to become embarrassed or defensive. I have found that organizational function is a significant part of team norms. Professions such as engineering and medicine, which are rooted in the scientific method, may value precision and logical reasoning more than other functions, for instance. To perform this step well, it's critical that you get curious about the other team's values and assumptions, instead of assuming you know the values or assumptions that explain the artifact. You can infer a team's culture from its artifacts, but you can't figure out whether your inference is correct without asking the team's members.

Finally, determine whether each artifact is shared, different but congruent, or conflicting. Conflicting artifacts are the most important to address because they present the greatest challenge to working together effectively.

Jointly design a solution for the different and conflicting values and assumptions

Focusing on the values and assumptions rather than on the artifacts is important both because it helps everyone understand the reasons behind each team's artifacts and because it helps you design solutions for norms, structures, and processes that are based on the same values and assumptions.

There are several options for designing a solution. If one team is particularly bound to its values and assumptions in a certain situation, the other team may decide simply to adopt that team's approach. For example, the team that discusses conflict privately may begin doing it in meetings if the other team makes a compelling case for it. Or the teams can develop a solution that integrates their cultures when the two are not necessarily incompatible. For example, the teams could agree to initially raise a conflict in private with the person who is most involved in solving it, and then jointly raise the issue with the larger team. Lastly, the teams can compromise when other options don't work. This may be the best solution you can develop, but because compromises don't resolve conflicting values and assumptions, they tend to leave everyone somewhat dissatisfied, so they may not create sustainable solutions. For example, the teams might agree to let each member decide on whether to raise a conflict privately or in the team.

Just as an effective team invests time and effort agreeing on how members will work together, so do teams that work effectively with each other.

———————

Roger Schwarz is an organizational psychologist, speaker, leadership team consultant, and president and CEO of Roger Schwarz & Associates. He is the author of *Smart Leaders, Smarter Teams: How You and Your Team Get Unstuck to Get Results*.

CHAPTER 11

Get Your Team to Do What It Says It's Going to Do

by Heidi Grant

Say you're in the early stages of planning your department's budget for the next fiscal year. Your management team meets to establish short-term priorities and starts to think about longer-term resource allocation. You identify next steps and decide to reconvene in a week—but when you do, you find that very little progress has been made. What's the holdup? Your to-dos probably look something like this:

Adapted from an article in *Harvard Business Review*, May 2014 (product #R1405E).

Step 1: Develop a tentative budget for continuing operations

Step 2: Clarify the department's role in upcoming corporate initiatives

Those steps may be logical, but they're ineffective because they omit essential details. Even the first one, which is relatively straightforward, raises more questions than it answers. What data must the team gather to estimate requirements for continuing operations? Who will run the reports, and when? Which managers can shed additional light on resource needs? Who will talk to them and reconcile their feedback with what the numbers say? When will that happen? Who will assess competing priorities and decide which trade-offs to make? When?

Creating goals that teams and organizations will actually accomplish isn't just a matter of defining what needs doing; you also have to spell out the specifics of getting it done, because you can't assume that everyone involved will know how to move from concept to delivery. By using what motivational scientists call if-then planning to express and implement your group's intentions, you can significantly improve execution.

If-then plans work because contingencies are built into our neurological wiring. Humans are very good at encoding information in "If x, then y" terms and using those connections (often unconsciously) to guide their behavior. When people decide exactly when, where, and how they will fulfill their goals, they create a link in their brains between a certain situation or cue ("If or when x happens") and the behavior that should follow ("then I will do y"). In this way, they establish powerful triggers for action.

We've learned from more than 200 studies that if-then planners are about 300% more likely than others to reach their goals. Most of that research focuses on individuals, but we're starting to uncover a similar effect in groups. Several recent studies indicate that if-then planning improves team performance by sharpening groups' focus and prompting members to carry out key activities in a timely manner.

That's an important finding, because organizations squander enormous amounts of time, money, ideas, and talent in pursuit of poorly expressed goals. If-then planning addresses that pervasive problem by sorting out the fine-grained particulars of execution for group members. It pinpoints conditions for success, increases everyone's sense of responsibility, and helps close the troublesome gap between knowing and doing.

Overcoming Obstacles to Execution

Peter Gollwitzer, the psychologist who first studied if-then planning (and my postdoctoral adviser at New York University), has described it as creating "instant habits." Unlike many of our other habits, these don't get in the way of our goals but help us reach them. Let's look at a simple work example.

Suppose your employees have been remiss in submitting weekly progress reports, and you ask them all to set the goal of keeping you better informed. Despite everyone's willingness, people are busy and still forget to do it. So you ask them each to make an if-then plan: "If it's 2 p.m. on Friday, I will email Susan a brief progress report."

Now the cue "2 p.m. on Friday" is directly wired in their brains to the action "email my report to Susan"—and it's just dying to get noticed. Below their conscious awareness, your employees begin to scan the environment for it. As a result, they will spot and seize the critical moment ("It's 2 p.m. on Friday") *even when busy doing other things.*

Once the "if" part of the plan is detected, the mind triggers the "then" part. People now begin to execute the plan without having to think about it. When the clock hits 2 on Friday afternoon, the hands automatically reach for the keyboard. Sometimes you're aware that you are following through. But the process doesn't have to be conscious, which means you and your employees can still move toward your goal while occupied with other projects.

This approach worked in controlled studies: Participants who created if-then plans submitted weekly reports only 1.5 hours late, on average. Those who didn't create them submitted reports eight hours late.

The if-then cue is really important—but so is specifying what each team member will do and when (and often where and how). Let's go back to the budgeting example. To make it easier for your team to execute the first step, developing a tentative budget for continuing operations, you might create if-then plans along these lines:

When it's Monday morning, Jane will detail our current expenses for personnel, contractors, and travel.

If it's Monday through Wednesday, Surani and David will meet with the managers in their groups to get input on resource needs.

When it's Thursday morning, Phil will write a report that synthesizes the numbers and the qualitative feedback.

When it's Friday at 2 p.m., the management team will reassess priorities in light of Phil's report and agree on trade-offs.

Now there's less room for conflicting interpretations. The tasks and time frames are clearly outlined. Individuals know what they're accountable for, and so do the others in the group.

Does the if-then syntax feel awkward and stilted? It might, since it doesn't reflect the way we naturally express ourselves. But that's actually a good thing, because when we articulate our goals more "naturally," the all-important details of execution don't stick. The if-then construction makes people more aware and deliberate in their planning, so they not only understand but also complete the needed tasks.

Solving Problems That Plague Groups

Beyond helping managers get better results from their direct reports, if-then planning can address some of the classic challenges that groups face when working and making decisions together. Members often allow cognitive biases to obscure their collective judgment, for example, falling into traps such as groupthink and fixation on sunk costs. New findings suggest that if-then planning can offer effective solutions to this class of problems.

Groupthink

In theory, teams should be better decision makers than individuals, because they can benefit from the diverse knowledge and experience that each member brings. But they rarely capitalize on what each person distinctively has to offer. Rather than offering up unique data and insights, members focus on information that they all possess from the start. Many forces are at work here, but primary among them is the desire to reach consensus quickly and without conflict by limiting the discussion to what's familiar to everyone.

Even when team members are explicitly told to share all relevant information with one another—and have monetary incentives to do so—they still don't. When people are entrenched in existing habits, paralyzed by cognitive overload, or simply distracted, they tend to forget to execute general goals like this.

Research by J. Lukas Thürmer, Frank Wieber, and Peter Gollwitzer conducted at the University of Konstanz demonstrates how if-then plans improve organizational decision making through increased information exchange and cooperation. In their studies, teams worked on "hidden profile" problems—which required members to share knowledge to identify the best solution. For instance, in one study, three-person panels had to choose the best of three job applicants. Candidate A was modestly qualified, with six out of nine attributes in his favor—but every panel member knew about all six attributes. Candidate B also had six attributes in his favor, but every panel member knew about three of them, and each had unique knowledge of one additional attribute. Candidate C, the superior candidate, had nine out of nine attributes in his favor, but each panel member received information about only three attributes. To realize that Candidate C had all nine, the members of a panel had to share information with one another.

All the panels were instructed to do so before coming to a final decision and were told that reviewing the bottom two candidates' positive attributes would be a good way to accomplish this. Half the panels made an if-then plan: "If we are ready to make a decision, then we will review the positive qualities of the other candidates before deciding." (All study participants knew that the if-then plans applied specifically to them—and that the task needed to be done at that moment—so they didn't spell out the who and the when as they would have in real life.)

A panel that focused only on commonly held information would choose Candidate A—one of the inferior candidates—reasoning that he had six attributes as opposed to Candidate B's four and Candidate C's three. A panel whose members broke free of groupthink and successfully shared information would realize that in fact Candidate C had all nine attributes and choose him instead.

Not surprisingly, panels that made no if-then plan chose the superior candidate only 18% of the time. Panels with if-then plans were much more likely to make the right decision, selecting the superior candidate 48% of the time.

Clinging to lost causes

Further studies by Wieber, Thürmer, and Gollwitzer show that if-then plans can help groups avoid another common problem: committing more and more resources to clearly failing projects.[1] As the Nobel Laureate Daniel Kahneman and his collaborator Amos Tversky pointed out decades ago, we tend to chase sunk costs—the time, effort, and money that we have put into something and can't get back out. It's irrational behavior. Once your team realizes that a project is failing, previous investments shouldn't matter. The best you can do is try to make smart choices with what you have left to invest. But too often we stay the course, unwilling to admit we have squandered resources that would have been better spent elsewhere. Groups, especially, tend to hang in there when it would be best to walk away, sometimes doubling down on their losing wagers. And the more cohesive they are, the greater the risk.[2]

The dangers of identifying too much with one's team or organization are well documented: pressure to conform, for instance, and exclusion of atypical group members from leadership positions. When being a "good" team member is all that matters, groups often (implicitly or explicitly) discourage diverse ways of thinking, and they're loath to acknowledge their imperfections and errors of judgment. Hence the blind spot when it comes to sunk costs.

However, by taking the perspective of an independent observer, a group can gain the objectivity to scale back on its commitments to bad decisions or cut its losses altogether. In other words, by imagining that some other team made the initial investment, people free themselves up to do what's best in light of current circumstances, not previous outlays.

Wieber, Thürmer, and Gollwitzer hypothesized that if-then planning might be a particularly good tool for instilling this mindset, for two reasons. First, studies showed that if-then plans helped individuals change strategies for pursuing goals, rather than continue with a failing approach. Second, additional research by Gollwitzer demonstrated that making if-then plans helped people take an outsider's view (they assumed the perspective of a physician when seeing blood in order to reduce feelings of disgust).

To test the effectiveness of if-then plans in scaling back group commitments, a study led by Wieber put subjects into teams of three and asked them to make joint investment decisions. Each team acted as a city council, deciding how much to invest in a public preschool project. During phase one the groups received information casting the project in a very positive light, and they allocated funds accordingly. In phase two they received both positive and negative information: Construction had begun and a local store was donating materials, but the building union wanted a substantial raise and environmental activists had voiced concerns about the safety of the land. Rationally, the teams should have begun to decrease funding at this point, given the uncertainty of the project's success. Finally, in phase three, the groups received mostly negative information: Oil had been found in the sand pit, parents were outraged, and fixing the problems would be time-consuming and expensive. Further scaling back was clearly called for.

So what did the teams do? Those that had made no if-then plans showed the typical pattern of commitment. They slightly increased the percentage of budget allocated to the project from phase one to phase three. In contrast, teams with if-then plans ("If we make a decision, we will take the perspective of a neutral observer that was not responsible for any prior investments") reduced their investments from phase one to phase three by 13%, on average. When teams or organizations set goals, they tend to use sweeping, abstract language. But it's easier to frame your plans in if-then terms if you first break them down into smaller, more concrete subgoals and then identify the actions required to reach each subgoal. (See figure 11-1.)

If you were trying to improve your team's communication, for example, you might set "Reduce information overload among staff members" as one subgoal. And after some brainstorming, you might decide to accomplish that by asking members who are forwarding any email to explain up front why they're doing so. (The rationale: People will be more selective about what they pass along if they have to provide a reason.) The if-then plan for each team member would be "If I forward any email, I'll include a brief note at the top describing what it is and why I'm sharing it." One manager I spoke with found that this if-then plan put an immediate end to the knee-jerk forwarding that had clogged everyone's inbox with unnecessary information. It also increased the value of the emails that people did forward.

FIGURE 11-1

How to design if-then plans

This flowchart shows how to translate a high-level ambition (in this instance, better communication) into detailed plans for execution.

Step 1
Establish organizational goal.

Step 2
Break the goal down into specific, concrete subgoals.

Step 3
Identify detailed actions—and the who, when, and where—for reaching each subgoal.

Step 4
Create if-then plans that trigger the actions.

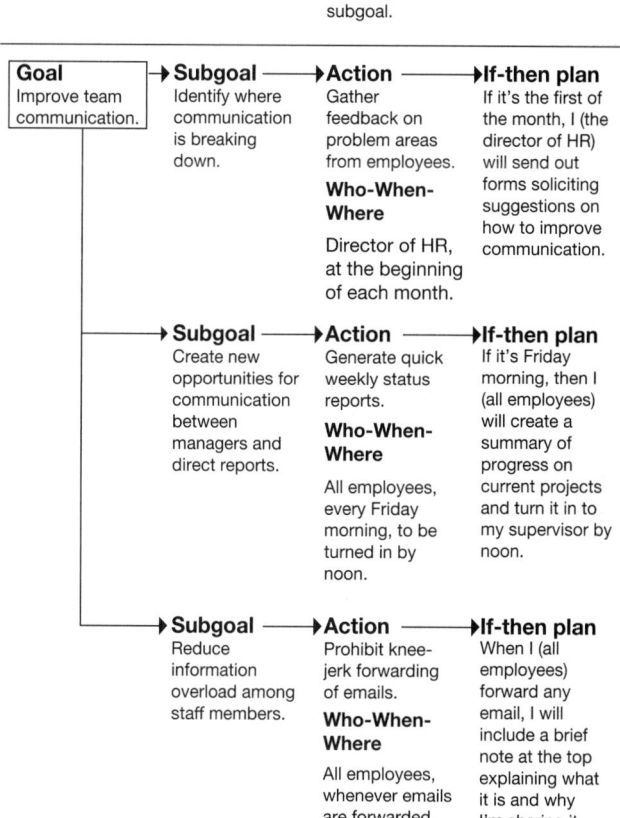

Goal Improve team communication.	**Subgoal** Identify where communication is breaking down.	**Action** Gather feedback on problem areas from employees. **Who-When-Where** Director of HR, at the beginning of each month.	**If-then plan** If it's the first of the month, I (the director of HR) will send out forms soliciting suggestions on how to improve communication.
	Subgoal Create new opportunities for communication between managers and direct reports.	**Action** Generate quick weekly status reports. **Who-When-Where** All employees, every Friday morning, to be turned in by noon.	**If-then plan** If it's Friday morning, then I (all employees) will create a summary of progress on current projects and turn it in to my supervisor by noon.
	Subgoal Reduce information overload among staff members.	**Action** Prohibit knee-jerk forwarding of emails. **Who-When-Where** All employees, whenever emails are forwarded.	**If-then plan** When I (all employees) forward any email, I will include a brief note at the top explaining what it is and why I'm sharing it.

Specifying the who, when, and where is an ongoing process, not a onetime exercise. Ask team members to review their if-then plans regularly. Studies[3] show that rehearsing the if-then link can more than double its effectiveness. It also allows groups to periodically reassess how realistic their plans are. Is anything harder or taking longer than expected? Are there steps that the team didn't plan for? If circumstances change, your if-then plans need to change, too—or they won't have the desired impact.

Though the research on if-then planning for teams and organizations is relatively new, the early results are promising, and social psychologists are examining several uses and benefits. (For instance, I'm studying whether it can be used to shift group mindsets from what I call "be good" thinking to "get better" thinking that fosters continuous improvement.) What's already becoming clear is that if-then planning helps groups frame their goals in a way that's achievable, providing a bridge between intentions and reality. It enables them to do more of what they mean to—and do it better—by fostering ownership and essentially reprogramming people to execute.

———————

Heidi Grant is a social psychologist who researches, writes, and speaks about the science of motivation. She is director of learning research and development for EY Americas and serves as associate director of Columbia's Motivation Science Center. She received her doctorate in social psychology from Columbia University. Her most recent book is *Reinforcements: How to Get People to Help You* (Harvard Business Review Press, 2018). She's also the author of *Nine Things Successful People Do Differently* (Harvard Business Review Press, 2018) and *No One Understands You and What to Do About It* (Harvard Business Review Press, 2015).

NOTES

1. Frank Wieber, J. Lukas Thürmer, and Peter Gollwitzer, "Collective Action Control by Goals and Plans," *American Journal of Psychology* 125, no. 3 (2012): 275–290, http://www.ncbi.nlm.nih.gov/pubmed/22953688.

2. Dustin Sleesman et al., "Cleaning Up the Big Muddy: A Meta-Analytic Review of the Determinants of Escalation of Commitment," *Academy of Management Journal* 55, no. 3 (2012), http://amj.aom.org/content/55/3/541.

3. Peter Gollwitzer and Paschal Sheeran, "Implementation Intentions and Goal Achievement," *Advances in Experimental Psychology* 38 (2006): 69–119, http://www.sciencedirect.com/science/article/pii/S0065260106380021.

CHAPTER 12

Don't Let Teamwork Get in the Way of Agility

by Elaine D. Pulakos and Robert B. (Rob) Kaiser

Effective teamwork has never been more important than it is today, as organizations face an exceedingly volatile economy with significant business threats. Prevailing wisdom would have us use teamwork as much as possible to face these challenges head-on. The theory is that working in teams—especially those with different skill sets and backgrounds—sparks innovation, enables agility, and leads to better outcomes. However, our recent research suggests that maximizing teamwork often fails

---

Adapted from content posted on hbr.org, May 12, 2020 (product #H05M3V).

to yield the results we expect; in fact, in some cases, it undermines them.[1]

The reality is that productive teamwork and collaboration are hard to achieve. Bringing together people with diverse expertise can potentially stall rather than fuel innovation, especially when responding to an urgent need. Not to mention the larger, structural tensions that often leave team members jockeying for positions, making power grabs, and withholding information to protect their turf.

This is not to say we should throw teamwork out the window entirely. Rather, we believe a change in mindset about how to best implement it is needed to achieve the agility and resilience that are vital for thriving in your career.

Instead of maximizing teamwork, our research on what distinguishes agile organizations suggests that we need to *rightsize* it.[2] This means considering what form and how much teamwork is needed at each stage of a project to get it done efficiently and effectively. Rightsizing teamwork requires judiciously selecting the right people to contribute, at the right time.

While this approach may initially seem in conflict with goals of inclusivity, consideration, and respect, when done right, it can improve those things. Involving others when they are needed, as opposed to by default, is actually *more* considerate and respectful of the many people who are suffering from project overload and burnout. Rightsizing is not about minimizing inclusion. It's about changing "teamwork" from a buzzword to an optimized practice that creates seamless companywide connections.

We believe organizations that master rightsizing will have a greater chance of success in this new business environment. The most agile companies do so by using three evidence-based practices:[3]

Define what kind of teamwork needs to take place

Different stages of work require different kinds of teamwork. For example, successfully completing tasks in the early production stage of a new initiative involves activities and requirements that differ from those needed in the final stage. There is no one-size-fits-all definition of what "good teamwork" looks like throughout a single project. More is not always better and, sometimes, *less* or even *none* is best. It's helpful to think of teamwork in four broad categories:

1. Sometimes teamwork is nothing more than a *handoff*. In this case, each person's work is mostly independent, but at the right point in time, one person needs to pass information or resources to another in order to complete a task. This type of teamwork relies on clear communication and coordination to help everyone involved understand what is needed and when. A good example is when different business units within a company provide monthly financial results to the corporate finance department, which then consolidates

them into a monthly financial report for the executive team and board members.

2. Other projects require *synchronized work*. This is when two or more separate teams (or individual contributors) perform the same routine but must remain coordinated in their work to reach a successful outcome. An example is a regional sales team. Each member prospects, closes, and manages their own customers using the same process. While each person works independently, the sum of everyone's work determines the regional team's success.

3. In some cases, a project requires *coordinated work*. People perform independent roles that impact each other. An example is the heroic critical care teams that worked throughout the Covid-19 crisis. These teams consist of different specialists—physicians, pharmacists, dieticians, respiratory therapists, and nurses—each of whom perform their own clearly defined tasks to achieve a team outcome.

4. Lastly, some projects require truly *interdependent work*, which is the most complex form of teamwork. An example is bringing a new product or innovation to market. People with different skills come together to solve a new problem. The team structure is often flexible and tends to take a more concrete shape as the problem is solved. As such, people are required to adjust their roles and

responsibilities on the fly in order to address and communicate through unpredictable situations. One example is a team we spoke to at Scripps Research. Members were charged with evaluating whether their program focused on developing health detection devices could be reengineered to test for Covid-19 cases. Unlike the other teams at Scripps, which use well-defined playbooks and have narrow roles, this new project required putting together a group of people who wear many hats and pitch in as needed.

Sometimes a team's work easily fits into one category. But more often—especially for teams involved in knowledge work, innovation, and repositioning their business—this is not true. What "good teamwork" means can change from project to project and even within projects as they evolve.

Given this, leaders across an organization can use the above categories to help develop a shared understanding of what type of teamwork needs to get done and when, including exactly who needs to collaborate, in what configuration, and why. This practice forces those handing out assignments to think of teamwork as something beyond "working together." Instead, it asks them to contextualize what good teamwork means in a given situation.

Simplify and then simplify some more

Rightsizing teamwork is an exercise in simplicity. To solve problems and overcome business challenges, leaders need to strike a balance between engaging those whose contribution is vital and boldly cutting out the people and processes that bog work down. This requires distinguishing what should be taken on as individual work versus what requires a team effort. For some, this might mean sunsetting that update meeting in lieu of an email or assigning the problem to two people who can solve it as opposed to dividing it among all six members of a team.

A simplification strategy we've seen work well is for leaders to ask one individual to get as far as they can collecting information and creating plans or draft materials at the start of a project. The rationale for this approach is based on the idea that it is more efficient for one person to create a draft that others can review than for multiple people to try and create a draft together. As the project evolves, the leader and assigned team member decide if others' input is needed and when, carefully planning what to ask and how to handle the feedback they receive.

However, just as there is no one way to define "good teamwork," there is no one-size-fits-all strategy for simplifying it. The strategy we offer works when one person can in fact produce an initial plan alone, as is often the case with a handoff or synchronized work. This strategy works less well when different types of expertise are needed from the start, as in the case of interdependent work.

The key to defining the best strategy for a given team involves taking a few structured steps:

- Analyze work requirements in terms of the four categories to determine what type of teamwork is needed or if none is needed.

- Decide what needs to be done by whom prior to convening your team. Your guiding principle is to make sure people's time is not wasted. Ask yourself: Who should be involved, why, and when?

- Review your process regularly. If something doesn't add value, eliminate it. For example, if three people are working on a task that one or two can achieve as easily, reduce the number of team members involved. If a meeting is scheduled for an hour but everything is covered in 30 minutes, end the meeting. If you have the authority to make a decision, get input from the necessary stakeholders, rather than waiting for the entire group to weigh in.

Give people permission to say no

Today, we are experiencing so much rapid change that leaders cannot personally ensure every instance of teamwork is rightsized. This is why employees must similarly understand how to apply the approach. Igniting a needed behavioral shift among team members may require clear, simple, and even shocking communications to grab people's attention and provoke rethinking.

How can leaders start?

- Jump-start the process by giving team members explicit permission to say no to teamwork when they feel it is adding unnecessary complexity, confusion, or inefficiency.

- Leaders should continually challenge themselves and their teams to carefully consider how much and what type of teamwork is needed for effective performance of the task at hand and how this may change at different stages of the work. Remember that every single person on a team should be performing a clear, valuable, and needed role. If there is room on a team for people to be lazy and not contribute, then there are too any people on the team and the number should be reduced.

- Reinforce and solidify the importance of rightsizing by calling out and discussing real examples of how saying no to teamwork has helped the team achieve more agile and effective performance. This will help team members develop a more mindful and judicious understanding of teamwork and how it can be applied.

To achieve the agility and resilience your company needs, you'll have to avoid the dysfunction and inefficiencies teamwork frequently brings. Knowing how to rightsize teamwork and starting to teach it now is imperative to your success and your ability to prepare for whatever comes next.

Elaine D. Pulakos is CEO of PDRI and an expert in building organizational and team capabilities that translate into business growth. She is well-known for her research and writing on agility, resilience, and driving improved business outcomes. She has extensive global experience helping companies build these capabilities into their companies to increase their competitive advantage and performance.

Robert B. (Rob) Kaiser is president of Kaiser Leadership Solutions and an adviser, author, and expert on the subject of leadership. He has extensive global experience in executive development, executive assessment, and people analytics and as a strategic talent management adviser to CEOs and HR leaders. Rob is also the author of an innovative suite of tools for executive assessment and development, including the *Leadership Versatility Index*.

NOTES

1. Elaine D. Pulakos et al., "What Leads to Organizational Agility: It's Not What You Think," *Consulting Psychology Journal* 71, no. 4 (2019): 305–320.

2. Pulakos et al., "What Leads to Organizational Agility."

3. Pulakos et al., "What Leads to Organizational Agility."

CHAPTER 13

How to Motivate Your Problem People

by Nigel Nicholson

Everyone knows that good managers motivate with the power of their vision, the passion of their delivery, and the compelling logic of their reasoning. Add in the proper incentives, and people will enthusiastically march off in the right direction.

It's a great image, promoted in stacks of idealistic leadership books. But something is seriously wrong with it: Such a strategy works with only a fraction of employees and a smaller fraction of managers. Why?

Adapted from an article in *Harvard Business Review*, January 2003 (product #R0301D).

For one thing, few executives are particularly gifted at rallying the troops. Exhorting most managers to become Nelson Mandelas or Winston Churchills imbues them with little more than a sense of guilt and inadequacy. For another, all available evidence suggests that external incentives—be they pep talks, wads of cash, or even the threat of unpleasant consequences—have limited impact. The people who might respond to such inducements are already up and running. It's the other folks who are the problem. And, as all managers know from painful experience, when it comes to managing people, the 80-20 rule applies: The most intractable employees take up a disproportionate amount of one's time and energy.

So how do you get these people to follow your lead? How do you get them energized and committed in such a way that they not only support your initiatives but carry them out?

After 30 years of studying business organizations and advising executives, I have concluded that these are precisely the wrong questions to ask. That's because, as it turns out, you can't motivate these problem people: Only they themselves can. Your job is to create the circumstances in which their inherent motivation—the natural commitment and drive that most people have—is freed and channeled toward achievable goals. That approach requires an entirely different managerial mindset. Achieving this shift in perspective is anything but easy. But it's your best hope for getting the most out of your difficult employees. And if you succeed, your task won't be prodding or coaxing these people; it will be removing barriers—including, quite possibly, your own demotivating management style.

A Familiar Problem

Let's look at a couple of situations that will surely resonate with most managers. First, consider the problem facing Annette. (Though the cases in this article are real, the names and identifying details have been changed.) She is a senior designer at a large publishing and graphic design business, with dotted-line responsibility for Colin, a project team member. Always something of a maverick, Colin nonetheless has a good work history. But the team is feeling the heat because the company restructured it to reduce costs and speed turnaround times. And Colin's behavior is becoming increasingly problematic, or so Annette and Dave, the project manager and Colin's other boss, see it. Colin seems to be shirking work, and when he does complete assignments, he doesn't report back to his bosses. To Annette, Colin's behavior doesn't just reflect his inherent disregard for rules and procedures; it also signifies a reluctance to take on further assignments. After discussing the situation with Dave, Annette decides that she will be the one to talk to Colin because she has the better relationship with him.

Annette's strategy is to motivate Colin by appealing to his sense of responsibility to the project team. When she meets with him and tries to get him to accept this line of reasoning, Colin agrees to do what Annette wants. But she doesn't get the feeling that her argument has made any impact. In her opinion, Colin is in his comfort zone: He supports the other team members, even helps them to solve their problems, but he does so at the expense of fulfilling his own responsibilities. Annette wonders whether Colin has become a misfit in the new structure and will have to leave. Perhaps she should give him a formal warning at his annual appraisal. Or maybe she should transfer him to a less demanding job, in effect demoting him.

Here's another case. Paolo works in Eastern Europe as a country manager for an international property developer. George, a chartered accountant with an MBA, is a direct report whose job is to sell plots of land and develop strategic alliances with local companies. George is fairly new to this position, having previously worked in a back-office role overseeing customer accounts. Although George is pleasant and enthusiastic, his performance is subpar and shows no signs of improvement. In fact, George has yet to sell a single parcel of land. In his dealings with potential partners, the garrulous George acts as though his bonhomie is all he needs to cut a deal. And the deals he does manage to make turn out to be ill considered and costly.

Because of these issues, Paolo meets with George several times to try to get him to change his ways. George responds with encouraging smiles, plausible excuses, and a commitment to Paolo that things will change, but nothing does. In the final analysis, Paolo decides, George is slippery and lazy. Despite his promises, George refuses to adopt a different negotiating style, and he obviously isn't prepared to do the detailed research necessary to appraise a deal. Exasperated, Paolo decides to issue George an ultimatum: Improve your game or get out.

But firing George would be an expensive option; people with his background and skills are difficult to find in this part of the world.

Poor Paolo. He can almost smell the failure likely to result from a confrontation. He'll continue to get reassurances from George, but will he ever get George to change his ways and be accountable for his performance? Poor Annette. If only she could convince Colin to improve his attitude, she could hold on to a potentially valuable team member. But no matter how reasonable Annette's argument is, will she be able to get Colin to behave differently?

The Mistakes Managers Make

These two cases share some qualities that often bedevil executives in their attempts to motivate problem people. For instance, Annette and Paolo believe that they just need the right sales pitch to turn around Colin and George. Each boss thinks, "If I can only get this person to listen, he'll see the logic of my position." This approach, something I call "tell and sell," is based on a profound fallacy many of us buy into: Other people have the same thought processes we do, and, consequently, they *have* to accept the good sense of what we're saying.

But each of us has a unique profile of motivational drivers, values, and biases, and we have different ideas about what is reasonable. This frequent mismatch of perceptions leads to another common problem with managerial attempts at motivation: the futile and prolonged game of tag, with a manager repeatedly trying to slap some motivation onto the problem employee. The

Being Productive as a Team

employee either evades the boss's attempts or, if tagged, quickly wriggles free. Think of Colin avoiding his bosses. Think of George and his elusive promises. Every manager is familiar with the "Sure, boss" meetings that end with an apparent resolution but ultimately result in more of the same old problem and the person not changing one jot.

In fact, such unsatisfactory outcomes shouldn't surprise managers like Annette and Paolo. In trying to convert Colin and George into different kinds of people, they—like most managers dealing with problem employees—have set themselves an impossible goal. A fundamental rule of management is that you can't change people's character; you can't even control their actions most of the time. Change comes from within or not at all.

A New Approach to Motivation

So if Annette and Paolo have approached their problems in the wrong way, what is the right way? I propose a relatively simple method I have seen work time and again. It involves shifting the responsibility for motivation from subject to object, from boss to subordinate. Crucially, it also involves a shift in perspective: The manager needs to look at the employee not as a problem to be solved but as a person to be understood. My method is based on a handful of principles:

Everyone has motivational energy

Although many problem employees display a marked lack of drive and commitment in their jobs, these qualities are usually alive and well in other areas of their lives.

Certainly, not all people are going to feel the same passion for their work that they do for their hobbies or other outside interests. But it's a mistake to write off a problem employee as simply unmotivated. Most workers have the potential to engage with their work in a way that furthers managerial goals.

This energy is often blocked in the workplace

A variety of factors can block people's natural motivation. For example, impediments may appear suddenly because of new stresses at home or may accumulate incrementally over years, the product of frustrated dreams or broken promises at work. The effect is to transform a person's positive energy into negative attitudes and behavior—or simply to divert it into nonwork activities. One of the most common blockages occurs when employees feel that their bosses don't really care about them. For this or other reasons, problem employees usually don't much like their managers. And chances are that the sentiments are mutual—which makes conventional pep talks about improving performance come across as insincere, at best.

Removing blockages requires employee participation

To motivate an employee to work toward your goals, you need to take a judolike approach: Find the person's locus of energy and leverage it to achieve your ends. Instead of pushing solutions on people with the force of your argument, pull solutions out of them. Turning the tables gets employees' attention at the very least; ideally, it prompts them to clear the obstacles impeding their motivation. To accomplish this, you may have to rethink what your problem employees can reasonably be motivated to do. But the approach will help you get the best from them, whatever their abilities and skills.

Let's look at potential objections to the method I'm proposing. "This all sounds too soft and squishy to me," you might say. Or, "I've got a business to run and have neither the inclination nor the time to serve as the sympathetic shrink to a bunch of 'blocked' employees who refuse to get with the program."

First, while this method is based on empathy, it is anything but soft. It demands that a manager take charge of a difficult situation and resolve it. In fact, the truly spongy method is what you are probably using now: either ignoring your problem employees or repeatedly and unsuccessfully trying to convince them that they should improve their performance. Although in exasperation you may end up sacking them, that's a sign of failure, not firmness. Second, my method does require an investment of time, but it is an investment that should get you to a resolution of the problem sooner than other means would. That's because it requires you to move beyond the point of "stuckness" that characterizes so many relationships with problem people.

Keep in mind that this approach is designed to create a resolution—not necessarily a solution—to the problem you face. While the method should help you avoid some common pitfalls in trying to motivate difficult employees, you won't be able to transform every unmotivated employee. And even if an employee's behavior does change, you may not get exactly what you originally wanted. But the three-step method I propose will put an end to the evasions, repetitions, and broken promises. And it will likely yield options that you hadn't even considered. At the very least, it will drive you to a moment of truth, a point at which you and the employee together can see a path to the goal you have set—or agree that no solution is possible.

Step 1: Create a Rich Picture

Tom has been struggling to help Jack improve his performance. But with each warning, Jack, who is naturally shy, just seems to get quieter. In the end, without fuss or ceremony, Tom tells Jack that things aren't working out and he'll have to leave the company. In the days that follow, Jack's former colleagues are abuzz with talk about his sudden dismissal—and what they've just learned about his situation. It turns out that both of Jack's parents had recently died after lingering and debilitating illnesses. Until now, no one, including Tom, knew what he had been going through.

Jack's case is extreme, but it illustrates a phenomenon distressingly common in business. A problem employee is taken through the usual appraisal routines and management discussions and then is dismissed—sometimes after years of unproductive performance. Shortly thereafter, the line manager learns from the person's former peers about something that may have been behind the poor performance. The manager never knew about it because of the employee's pride or natural reserve—or because the individual disliked or mistrusted the manager.

The first step thus requires that a manager work to understand where a problem employee is coming from: What drives that person? What blocks those drives? What might happen if the impediments are removed? But that isn't all. Two other factors also figure in the equation: you, as the boss, and the context within which the problem is occurring.

Let's start with the employee. How can Tom know so little about what is affecting Jack's work? How well does Annette understand Colin? What does Paolo really know about George? Clearly, these managers need more information. It can come from peers, subordinates, or previous bosses. Much of the data will come, however, from problem employees themselves. You need to have a series of informal conversations—at the water cooler, over lunch, at social events—that will give you insight into what your employees are really about. What does the world look like from where the employee sits? How have his expectations and desires been molded by key past experiences? What passions govern his choices? What stifles these passions in the workplace? This may sound difficult, but in executive classes I teach, I find that people can learn these things about one another in a 10-minute interview, if they ask the right questions. After all, we often have these conversations at dinner parties; we just rarely have them at work. What you discover will likely surprise you. A test of this would be asking problem employees to describe themselves. It's almost a certainty that they would use different words from the ones you might use.

These informal conversations are the starting point in effectively motivating problem people. For example, Annette learns through some asking around that Colin, outside work, is building a house. No motivation problem there!

Next, you need to look at your own role in the problem you've been trying to solve, especially because direct bosses are the most potent source of employee dissatisfaction and the chief reason people quit their jobs. In fact, you may be the main, if inadvertent, cause of your employee's lack of motivation; for one reason or another, you are bringing out the worst rather than the best in the person you're trying to help. You will have to do some honest soul-searching. And you'll need to do the same sort of asking around that helped you fill out your picture of the employee. Your problem employee may be uncomfortable talking about his or her perception of you, but over time you may even be able to piece together a picture—probably unflattering—of how you are viewed. Even if that picture seems unfair and inaccurate, remember: If something is perceived as real, it is real in its consequences.

Others can provide additional information. Paolo, in discussing George with another manager, complains: "He acts like I'm persecuting him, if you can believe that." Imagine Paolo's surprise when the colleague, who is a friend, responds, "Well, Paolo, I'm sure he's wrong about persecution, but you do come across as a bit of a bully sometimes."

What you learn may convince you that your relationship with the problem employee is dysfunctional beyond repair, at which point you should abandon the method and hand over the motivation task to someone else. More likely, though, the way you interact with a problem employee—for example, something as basic as the way you talk to that person—is simply a turn-off. What works fine with your other reports is hopelessly wrong for this individual. Needless to say, that can be a chastening realization, and many managers find it hard to face.

Finally, you need to analyze the context. Is something about the current situation bringing out the worst in the employee—and maybe in you? Annette thinks Colin's performance has deteriorated because of the increased demands the restructuring has placed on the project team. But Annette's under pressure, too. Are Colin's actions bothering Annette more than they would otherwise because of the stress she faces? Do her reactions to him, paradoxically, add to Colin's stress, creating a vicious cycle?

Once you embark on this kind of fact-finding mission, you'll see that you didn't have sufficient data to solve your problem. Quite possibly, your dislike has gotten in the way of getting to know the problem employee. Furthermore, you probably didn't think your own behavior could be partly to blame. And you probably haven't gone out of your way to look for situational factors that might in some sense excuse the employee's shortcomings. It's much easier simply to label people as difficult than to figure out how they got that way or implicate yourself in the mess.

But if you can break out of this narrow mindset, you're more likely to get the employee to perform better. And you'll probably rethink what you wanted to achieve with this problem employee in the first place.

Step 2: Reframe Your Goals

Hans runs a division of a Swiss brokerage business. Luca is a member of a 12-person back-office team there that, although it processes customer accounts, has little customer contact. Luca's team is split into two factions, the result of his rumormongering and abysmal relations with the group's secretary—or so Hans believes. Hans doesn't particularly like Luca, who is very different from Hans: Luca is physically imposing, working class, a big spender who loves flashy cars and always seems to have money problems. Luca seems to feel similar antipathy toward Hans.

Although Luca's performance on the job isn't bad, Hans believes that Luca could achieve more, and improve overall group performance, if he spent less time gossiping and cultivated a better relationship with the secretary. He has casually mentioned this to Luca several times, to no avail, and Hans is ready to get rid of him. But from an informal poll of Luca's coworkers, Hans learns that most don't want him to go, despite the trouble he seems to cause. So Hans decides to confront Luca and demand that he get along with the secretary and stop playing office politics.

You may know firsthand the frustration that Hans feels: "I'm a reasonable person, trying to do a good job, facing an unreasonable person who refuses to acknowledge what is clearly the right and sensible way to solve this problem. I've told him what needs to be done. Why can't he *just do it*?" If you are faced with this situation, you're likely to simply give up, either by letting things drift or by firing the employee involved. Unfortunately, your moralizing stance and failure to realize that not everyone sees things the way you do will limit both your chances of successfully motivating the employee and the options you consider for solving the problem. You'll be better served if you let go of your desire to bring a bad employee to justice—and instead determine what can be gained by rehabilitating a wayward one. You will be more effective if you are willing to switch from your predetermined solution to an array of possible outcomes.

In the case here, Hans believes the solution is to change Luca's behavior, which he sees as the source of the team's turmoil and Luca's poor performance. But if Luca is to blame for the team's problems, why aren't his coworkers eager for him to go? Hans decides to gather more information to enrich his picture of the situation. He learns that the team's lack of customer contact may be depriving Luca of the stimulus he needs for job satisfaction. Just as important, it may be engendering a "rats in a cage" atmosphere for the entire back-office team—an environment of infighting further poisoned by a recently introduced financial incentive scheme and Hans's neglect of team-building initiatives.

Viewed this way, Luca's behavior may be the effect rather than the cause of the problem. Once Hans begins to think about what makes Luca tick, he wonders whether Luca's natural proclivity toward gossip and office politics might be channeled into a positive social endeavor such as team building. Sure, Luca needs to rebuild bridges with the secretary—not to mention with Hans—but the true motivational challenge may be to co-opt Luca as an ally to improve the entire office's climate.

Let's be clear: Reframing your goals in this way doesn't represent capitulation. Yes, you sometimes may settle on more modest and achievable goals for your problem employee, ones that the individual will get behind and is capable of meeting. But a willingness to be flexible in your aims can also yield novel and ambitious alternatives you may not have considered. In the end, you may not get exactly what you wanted from the employee, but you'll certainly get more than you did before.

Putting together a menu of possible outcomes is a crucial prerequisite to scheduling a formal encounter with the employee that is designed to solve or resolve the situation. Keep in mind that this menu may be augmented with a solution from that unlikeliest of sources: the employee. At the same time, this is not an "anything goes" agenda. You should be clear about bottom-line sticking points: those issues that, if you don't arrive at a solution to the problem, will shape a resolution—possibly the employee's termination.

Step 3: Stage the Encounter

Jerry has recently been appointed a department head at a pharmaceuticals company. As he settles in, he discovers he has inherited one very troublesome subordinate. Bernard—like Jerry, in his mid-30s—is an extremely competent scientist and very independent minded. Bernard performs well enough when given a defined and highly complex piece of work that puts his technical expertise to the test. But he fails to discuss his results until it is too late for Jerry to provide his own input. And Bernard resists doing anything that departs from his accustomed routines. Jerry suspects that Bernard could do his work more quickly without sacrificing quality. But when Jerry raises the issue, Bernard snows him with technical explanations that Jerry doesn't fully understand.

Jerry learns that Bernard was once passed over for promotion and has had a bad attitude ever since. In fact, Bernard has made it plain to everyone that he resents having to report to someone he regards as his inferior in technical knowledge. Although Jerry thinks that Bernard should have been reined in long ago, he has attempted on numerous occasions to win over Bernard with friendly approaches. "What are you up to?" Jerry will ask. "You always seem to have such a creative approach to problems." But Bernard rebuffs him: "You'll never understand my work." Jerry is frustrated because he knows Bernard's considerable skills are not being fully used to benefit the business. And the growing animosity between the two men doesn't bode well for improving the situation.

Hoping to help Bernard improve his performance, Jerry has gone through the first step of the method presented here: piecing together a layered picture of the man and how his past experiences and current situation (not to mention Jerry's arrival) may have contributed to the problem. Jerry decides that Bernard feels a need to preserve his dignity, which was diminished when he was passed over for promotion. This trait is getting in the way of Bernard making an energetic commitment to working for Jerry. With this more nuanced understanding, Jerry takes the method's second step: reevaluating what he hopes to get out of Bernard. Jerry's own boss has advised him, as many bosses would, to assert his authority and tell Bernard to shape up or ship out. But Jerry knows that approach probably won't do much good. Instead, he hopes to motivate Bernard by leveraging his inherent desire for dignity, respect, and recognition. He would like Bernard to see that he is taking a self-defeating stance and that big personal rewards can be had from bringing these drives to bear on new challenges.

At the same time, Jerry knows he needs to be tougher than he has been. So he decides to undertake a focused, face-to-face encounter with Bernard. One positive by-product of Jerry's analysis of the situation is a certain detachment about Bernard: Jerry recognizes his own negative feelings—which have become increasingly intense in the face of Bernard's rudeness—but has put them aside before the encounter takes place. In fact, Jerry has even come to realize that he is part of the problem and that any positive outcome will almost assuredly require him to modify how he manages Bernard. If all goes well, Bernard, too, will begin to transform the way he views the situation.

This formal conversation with a problem employee, unlike the informal interactions you use to piece together a rich picture of the situation, is my method's third step. It should be a carefully staged event that underscores its importance. Hold the meeting on neutral ground—say, a conference room—and block out at least an hour for it. (In fact, it may take more than a single meeting, depending on how far you get in the first encounter.) You should tell the employee about it a day or so in advance, but emphasize that no materials or preparation are needed; this will not be a formal appraisal meeting but a chance to review and revise your working relationship. In fact, the only physical props you will need are a table and two chairs, set at a right angle.

The meeting opens with what I call an *affirmative assertion*, a brief "soft-hard" introduction. You affirm the employee's past and future value to the organization and express your desire for a mutually beneficial outcome to the meeting. But you also honestly describe the current problem as it looks to you and assert that things cannot and will not continue as they are now. For example, Jerry might say to Bernard:

"Thanks for meeting with me. I've been thinking about how we work together, and I have to tell you I'm not happy. My sense is that you aren't, either. I'm not exactly sure what the problem is. That's why I want us to talk now. I admire your talents and what you offer the company, but our previous conversations have shown me that we see our roles quite differently. I don't like the way you've responded to me on a number of occasions, but I realize you may feel the same way. I think you can help me to help us get on a different footing and identify new ways to work together. Certainly things can't go on the way they are—I won't let them."

You then need to engage in what I call *leverage questioning*. This is an intense and extended inquiry that tests hypotheses you have formulated in the course of developing your picture of the situation. Jerry's questions probe Bernard's need for recognition and ways in which it might be co-opted for productive ends. While one aim of such questions is to find unknown and potentially fruitful areas of agreement, they are also meant to bring differences into the open. In fact, one sign of a failed encounter—yet another "Sure, boss" meeting—is the employee managing to get out of the room without expressing a contrary view.

Care is needed here: It is very easy to slip back into telling and selling, shoveling facts and arguments onto the employee in order to bury that individual under the weight of the evidence. Even if you avoid this pitfall, the employee may still be evasive, defensive, hostile, or uncommunicative. Your goal is to discern in the haze of discontent the fleeting conversational windows that open up new views of the situation or offer opportunities to leverage your employee's driving passions.

For example, Jerry confronts Bernard on a sensitive issue: "Okay, I know you are technically superior to me. That's fine. So what do you think my role should be, then? What can I do to help you?"

Bernard doesn't hesitate in his response: "Nothing. Nobody around here with any technical smarts gets any respect anyway."

Jerry sees an opening: "Gee! Is that how you feel? Well, I guess I can see how that might have been a problem in the past. In fact, I understand why you were upset when you didn't get that promotion. But I value technical expertise. I think we could figure out how to put yours to better use—and in a way that would give you some credit for it."

The stage is set for the *moment of truth*. Jerry and Bernard have reached some agreement on at least part of the problem. And Jerry has brought Bernard to the point where he can help find a solution—one that plays to the qualities that motivate him. To return to the judo metaphor, Jerry has blocked Bernard by insisting that things will not continue as they are. Now Jerry will try to execute a throw, using Bernard's own energy as the impetus for movement toward Jerry's goals:

"Bernard. Thanks for being so open with me. I have a much better understanding of the issues as you see them. What you are saying suggests that your job might be restructured so you can do things that take fuller advantage of your exceptional talents. I'm thinking, for example, of high-profile advisory and coaching work for teams within our unit. I'd like you to come up with some concrete proposals about what form this work might take. I'll do the same, and we'll meet again in a week. Listen, we'd rather keep you than lose you. But continuing in your present position, at least as you have defined it, is not viable. What do you think?"

The Broader Benefits

Remember that the method I have described guarantees a resolution, not a solution, to a problem of the kind Jerry faces. To see the difference between these two outcomes, let's return to Annette and Paolo. In her encounter with Colin, Annette engages in a new kind of conversation, hoping to figure out what his drivers are and where they are being blocked. She concludes that he is highly motivated in other areas of his life but doesn't respond well to pressure. She sees that such pressure will only be heightened if she tries to make him feel guilty about letting down his team when it needs him most. He needs different, not greater, responsibility. When Annette probes to find out what really engages Colin, the key turns out to be helping others. How can this insight be used to motivate him? During their meeting, Colin raises the possibility of assuming a training role—one that he successfully migrates into during the subsequent months.

Paolo's case is trickier and doesn't have such a happy ending. The problem is resolved but not solved. Paolo's original goal was to get George to admit that he needed to be more accountable for his work. But after some thinking, Paolo decides he simply wants George to see that moving beyond the current situation is going to require making some difficult choices. They sit down together and Paolo offers specific data about George's performance. These hard facts help George realize that he's having a problem in his new position and admit that he isn't motivated to solve it. The two agree that the next step is for Paolo to help George move into a role with less customer contact. This does indeed happen—but without Paolo's help. Two weeks after their meeting, George accepts a job with another company. While Annette got a clear win, Paolo had to console himself that the outcome was better than the collision he had expected: George being fired and taking his rage and resentment with him to another employer. In fact, George ultimately was probably grateful for the new beginning that sprang from his moment of truth with Paolo.

Whether a problem is solved or simply resolved, the payoffs to be gained by using this method extend beyond the present situation and the individuals involved. Besides increasing your chances of motivating problem individuals, the method can help you motivate your entire work group.

Turning around a problem person boosts everyone's morale. One of the most common workplace complaints is that bosses don't deal with poor performers. Typically, successive bosses leave a problem person alone, shying away from the mixture of cost and futility they anticipate would come from any attempt to improve matters. So when the employee perks up and starts acting more reasonably, the outward ripples are palpable.

But it's not just that people now find it easier working with someone who once was a problem. Your efforts also send a strong message. When people want a boss to "deal with" a poor performer, that doesn't always mean outright dismissal. Recall Luca's coworkers, who resisted Hans's efforts to sack the troublemaker. In your efforts to turn someone around—even if you ultimately fail and the person quits—people will see the mark of a manager and a culture that prefer problem solving to waste disposal. Summarily getting rid of someone, on the other hand, signals that the organization discards rather than deals with difficult people—and who knows who might be next?

The benefits across your organization can themselves justify the demands of this method. Yes, it can be time-consuming, difficult, and fraught with risks and set-backs: Although some employees may respond quickly to your approach, others might require time to rebuild positive relationships with you and their work. But at least they will be heading in the right direction, under their own steam. And in the end, you ideally will have not only a rehabilitated employee but also a healthier, more productive organization.

Nigel Nicholson is a professor of organizational behavior at London Business School.

Communicating and Making Decisions

CHAPTER 14

Cracking the Code of Sustained Collaboration

by Francesca Gino

Ask any leader whether his or her organization values collaboration, and you'll get a resounding yes. Ask whether the firm's strategies to increase collaboration have been successful, and you'll probably receive a different answer.

"No change seems to stick or to produce what we expected," an executive at a large pharmaceutical company recently told me. Most of the dozens of leaders I've interviewed on the subject report similar feelings of

---

Adapted from an article in *Harvard Business Review*, November–December 2019 (product #R1906C).

frustration: So much hope and effort, so little to show for it.

One problem is that leaders think about collaboration too narrowly: as a value to cultivate but not a skill to teach. Businesses have tried increasing it through various methods, from open offices to naming it an official corporate goal. While many of these approaches yield progress—mainly by creating opportunities for collaboration or demonstrating institutional support for it—they all try to influence employees through superficial or heavy-handed means, and research has shown that none of them reliably delivers truly robust collaboration.

What's needed is a *psychological* approach. When I analyzed sustained collaborations in a wide range of industries, I found that they were marked by common mental attitudes: widespread respect for colleagues' contributions, openness to experimenting with others' ideas, and sensitivity to how one's actions may affect both colleagues' work and the mission's outcome. Yet these attitudes are rare. Instead, most people display the opposite mentality, distrusting others and obsessing about their own status. The task for leaders is to encourage an outward focus in everyone, challenging the tendency we all have to fixate on ourselves—what we'd like to say and achieve—instead of what we can learn from others.

Daunting as it may sound, some organizations have cracked this code. In studying them I've identified six training techniques that enable both leaders and employees to work well together, learn from one another, and overcome the psychological barriers that get in the way of doing both. They all help people connect more fully and consistently. They impress upon employees that there's a time to listen and explore others' ideas, a time to express their own, and a time to critique ideas and select the ones to pursue—and that conflating those discussions undermines collaboration.

1. Teach People to Listen, Not Talk

The business world prizes good self-presentation. Employees think a lot about how to make the right impression—how to frame their arguments in discussions with bosses, get their points across in meetings, persuade or coerce their reports to do what they want. (Many also spend serious money on speaking coaches, media trainers, and the like.) This is understandable, given the competitive nature of our workplaces, but it has a cost. My research suggests that all too often when others are talking, we're getting ready to speak instead of listening. That tendency only gets worse as we climb the corporate ladder.

We fail to listen because we're anxious about our own performance, convinced that our ideas are better than others', or both. As a result we get into conflicts that could be avoided, miss opportunities to advance the conversation, alienate the people who haven't been heard, and diminish our teams' effectiveness.

When we really listen, on the other hand, our egos and our self-involvement subside, giving everybody the space to understand the situation—and one another—and to focus on the mission. Listening can be improved by these practices:

Ask expansive questions

This is one of the behaviors encouraged at the animation studio Pixar. People stepping into managerial roles are required to take, among other courses, a 90-minute lunchtime class on the art of listening, which is held in a conference room decorated with posters of movie characters reminding participants to "Stay curious" and "Build on others' ideas."

In the class, participants discuss the qualities of great listeners they've known (such as generosity in acknowledging the points of others) and practice "active listening." That means suppressing the urge to interrupt or dominate a conversation, make it about yourself, or solve your conversation partners' problems, and instead concentrating on the implications of their words. In one exercise participants practice asking their partners open-ended "what" and "how" questions—which prompt people to provide more information, reflect on their situations, and feel more heard—rather than yes-or-no questions, which can kill conversations. For instance, instead of saying to someone "Did you try asking others who've worked on similar projects for advice?" participants are coached to ask "In what ways have you reached out to others for advice?"

Focus on the listener, not on yourself

In another exercise, two coaches act out conversations to illustrate the difference between active listening and not really listening. One coach might say: "I've been so sick, and our calendar is so full, and I have this trip planned to see my family. There's so much to do and I just don't know how I'm going to pull it all off." In the not-listening interaction, the other coach responds, "At least you get to go to Europe" or "I'm going to Croatia in two weeks, and I'm really excited." In the active-listening version, she says, "That sounds really stressful—like you'll feel guilty for leaving work and guilty if you don't visit your family." The coaches then ask the class to share their reactions and try the more effective approach in pairs.

Engage in "self-checks"

The American roofing-systems unit of Webasto, a global automotive-equipment manufacturer, has developed a good approach to raising employees' awareness. When Philipp Schramm became its CFO, in 2013, the unit's financial performance was in a downward spiral. But that was not its only problem. "Something was dysfunctional," recalls Schramm. "There was no working together, no trust, no respect." So in 2016 he introduced the Listen Like a Leader course, which features various exercises, some of which are similar to Pixar's.

Several times throughout the course participants engage in self-checks, in which they critique their own tendencies. People work in small groups and take turns sharing stories about times they've failed to listen to others and then reflect on common trends in all the stories.

The self-checks are reinforced by another exercise in which people pair up for multiple rounds of role-playing intended to help participants experience not being heard. One employee is told to describe an issue at work to the other. The listener is instructed to be inattentive during the first round, to parrot the speaker (repeat his or her statements) during the second, and to paraphrase the speaker (restate the message without acknowledging the speaker's feelings or perspective) during the third. Employees play both roles in each round. The idea is to demonstrate that hearing someone's words is not enough; you also need to take in the speaker's tone, body language, emotions, and perspective, and the energy in the conversation. At the end they discuss what that kind of listening can accomplish and how one feels when truly listened to.

Become comfortable with silence

This doesn't mean just not speaking; it means communicating attentiveness and respect while you're silent. And it's a challenge for those who are in love with the sound of their own voices. Such people dominate discussions and don't give others who are less vocal or who simply need more time to think an opportunity to talk.

In another exercise at Webasto, people sit in on a conversation simply to listen. They're instructed to avoid negative nonverbal behavior—such as rolling their eyes when they disagree with someone. The course motto "I am the message!" serves as a reminder to use positive body language when interacting with colleagues.

In successful collaborations, judgment gives way to curiosity

After taking the Listen Like a Leader class, employees have reported better interactions with their colleagues. Jeff Beatty, a program manager, reflected: "I thought leading was steamrolling people who got in your way—it was about aggressiveness and forcefulness. After going through the class, I can't believe that my wife has put up with me for 30 years."

2. Train People to Practice Empathy

Think about the last time you were in a conflict with a colleague. Chances are, you started feeling that the other person was either uncaring or not very bright, my research suggests. Being receptive to the views of someone we disagree with is no easy task, but when we approach the situation with a desire to understand our differences, we get a better outcome.

In successful collaborations, each person assumes that everyone else involved, regardless of background or title, is smart, caring, and fully invested. That mindset makes participants want to understand why others have differing views, which allows them to have constructive conversations. Judgment gives way to curiosity, and people come to see that other perspectives are as valuable as theirs. A couple of approaches can help here.

Expand others' thinking

At Pixar an exercise called "leading from the inside out" has participants present a relevant challenge to their collaborators on a project. Then their teammates ask questions but are instructed *not* to use them as a means of touting their own ideas. Instead, they're supposed to help the presenter think through the problem differently, without offering judgment about the presenter's perceptions or approach or those of other questioners.

If a presenter describes the challenge of getting a team member to speak up more often in brainstorming meetings, for instance, the questioners could ask, "How has his behavior changed?" or "Are there other contexts where this person is more talkative?" If questioners try to sneak in their ideas or opinions, a coach will ask them to rephrase their questions. "We realize that, though simple, these techniques are hard to implement on a regular basis," Jamie Woolf, Pixar's leadership development manager, who serves as one of the two main coaches, told me. "So, when someone is, consciously or not, trying to promote his or her point of view, we intervene so that we give the person an opportunity to apply the technique correctly and others the opportunity to learn."

With this approach, ideas get full attention and consideration. Creative solutions are generated, and team members feel that they've been truly heard.

Look for the unspoken

An advertising and publicity firm I studied uses a similar approach but also trains participants to pay attention to what people are *not* saying. If a member of the creative team presents an idea for how to shape an ad campaign to the client's needs, for instance, the colleagues listening are tasked with trying to understand his or her state of mind. During one session I observed, a colleague said to a presenter, "I noticed your voice was somewhat tentative, as if you were feeling uncertain about your idea. What are some of the strengths and weaknesses you see in it?"

When team members focus on conveying empathy more than on sharing their opinions, I've found, everyone feels more satisfied with the discussion. Showing empathy also makes others more likely to ask you for your point of view. Collaboration proceeds more smoothly.

While listening and empathizing allow others more space in a collaboration, you also need the courage to have tough conversations and offer your views frankly. The next three techniques focus on getting people there.

3. Make People More Comfortable with Feedback

Good collaboration involves giving and receiving feedback well—and from a position of influence rather than one of authority. The following methods can help.

Discuss feedback aversion openly

One of Pixar's classes trains new managers to provide feedback more often and effectively and also to get better at absorbing it. Coaches first explain that aversion to feedback is common. As givers of it, we want to avoid hurting others. (Even when we know our feedback can be helpful, my research has found, we choose not to provide it.) As recipients, we feel tension between the desire to improve and the desire to be accepted for who we are. The ensuing open discussion of reservations and challenges around feedback helps participants feel less alone.

Make feedback about others' behavior direct, specific, and applicable

At Pixar and other organizations, employees are asked to follow three rules for feedback: Be straightforward in both how you address a person and what you say about him or her; identify the particular behavior that worked (or didn't); and describe the impact of the behavior on you and others. These practices help counteract a common problem: People's feedback is too general. In an exercise Pixar designed to overcome it, participants are asked to think of a time when they might have offered positive feedback but didn't, and then write down what they *could* have said, following the three rules. Next they practice delivering that feedback to a classmate and reflect on the experience. (In another exercise they do the same with critical feedback.) Recipients are asked to talk about their experience getting the feedback.

Give feedback on feedback

In this exercise a volunteer reads a piece of feedback that he or she has drafted to the group. The other participants are then asked to identify ways to improve it. If the volunteer says, "You keep missing deadlines," for instance, the colleagues might suggest more specificity— perhaps "You missed three deadlines in the past month."

This practice is important because even when we overcome our aversion to giving feedback, we tend not to be specific or direct. As Pixar's Woolf told me, "Often leaders come to see me right before an important meeting they're about to have and say, 'Can I rehearse a bit more? I'm afraid of backpedaling and sugarcoating.' After some rehearsing they're able to walk into meetings with greater confidence and more clarity on how they'll say what they want to say."

Add a "plus" to others' ideas

Whenever a Pixar employee comments on a colleague's idea or work during a brainstorming session, he or she must offer a "plus"—a suggestion for an improvement that doesn't include judgment or harsh language. Pixar employees told me that this approach draws on three principles of improv comedy: First, accept all offers— that is, embrace the idea instead of rejecting it. Second, to ensure that you're building on someone's idea, say "Yes, and . . ." rather than "Yes, but . . ." Third, make your teammate look good by enhancing the scene or project he or she has started.

Provide live coaching

Though tactics like plussing are well understood at Pixar, it isn't always easy for employees at the company to put them into practice. For this reason, coaches there attend brainstorming meetings to reinforce good approaches and point out lapses. If a comment or a question doesn't show "collaborative spirit," the coach will ask that it be rephrased. Live coaching can be difficult—people are sometimes visibly annoyed by the interruptions—but coaches have learned to pay attention to the personalities in the room and adapt accordingly. For example, rather than asking a director to reframe a comment, a Pixar coach might ask him or her to describe the interaction that just occurred: what worked and what didn't. "In the moment the feedback may not feel good," Woolf told me. "As with medicine, it often takes a while for people to see the benefits. But they come to realize that feedback is a gift and is key to their personal development."

4. Teach People to Lead *and* Follow

A lot of attention is paid, in the literature and in the practice of management, to what makes a truly effective leader. There has been much less consideration of how to follow, though that, too, is an important skill. In interviews at American Express, I learned that the company's best collaborators—those known for adding value to interactions and solving problems in ways that left everyone better off—are adept at both leading and following, moving smoothly between the two as appropriate. That is, they're good at *flexing*.

During the 17-day campaign to find and rescue a group of boys and their soccer coach from a rapidly flooding cave in Thailand in 2018, more and more people arrived on the scene to help: hydraulic engineers, geologists, divers, SEAL teams, NASA experts, doctors, and local politicians. Only through flexing were these collaborators able to contribute all they could and get the most out of those around them. At one point, for example, an inexperienced engineer proposed an unorthodox plan to use large tubes on the mountain above the cave to divert some of the rainwater that was making diving unsafe. Rather than dismissing the idea, senior engineers flexed, giving it the consideration it deserved. After testing revealed the idea's promise, it was implemented, and the water stopped rising.

Because flexing requires ceding control to others, many of us find it difficult. A few simple exercises can make people more likely to flex:

Increase self-awareness

In some of my classes, I ask students to rate themselves relative to their classmates in three areas: their ability to make good decisions, their ability to get along well with others, and their honesty. Then I ask them to compute their average across the three. Most people's average is higher than 50% and typically in the 70th or 80th percentile, which demonstrates to the students how self-perceptions are often inflated. After all, it's impossible for a majority of respondents to merit better-than-average ratings across all three desirable dimensions. Unfortunately, our overly optimistic self-perceptions drive our decisions about whether to allow others to have control. So it helps to build self-awareness using this kind of exercise.

Learn to delegate

This isn't important just for leaders; it's also critical for people working on collaborations where multiple experts come together, such as the Thai cave rescue, and on cross-functional team projects. In a training session to help new Pixar managers delegate, participants discuss why it's so difficult to pass the torch to others and the main reasons we tend to micromanage: It's hard to let go of control, and we feel responsible for the outcome and are aware that the task needs to get done "right." So we focus on the short-term results rather than the long-term goal of developing others through delegation. We favor getting the job done—fast—over the reasons for delegating (allowing others to feel engaged and to grow, and allowing ourselves more time and probably higher productivity in the long run). The coaches talk about cases of delegation gone wrong—whose central lesson is the need for trust—and present a four-quadrant chart, the "skill-will model," which explains how to tailor delegation to the abilities and motivation of those being handed control.

5. Speak with Clarity and Avoid Abstractions

In any collaboration there are times for open discussion of ideas and times when someone, regardless of whether he or she is a leader, needs to cut through the confusion and clearly articulate the path forward. When we communicate with others, psychological research shows, we are often too indirect and abstract. Our words would carry more weight if we were more concrete and provided vivid images of goals. And our statements would also be judged more truthful.

Communication classes both at Pixar and at a large pharmaceutical company I studied included this role-playing exercise: Participants were instructed to think about something they needed to tell a team member and then ask themselves, "What am I trying to accomplish?" They were given time to practice their message. After they delivered it, the person playing the teammate told them whether they in fact had conveyed it with clarity and purpose. And if the teammate couldn't understand why the conversation was happening, the participant was prompted to ask why and then to reframe the statement to be clearer and more specific and include a purpose. Take a statement like "The project led by our marketing colleagues needs more resources and attention to get to the finish line." That might be revised as "The project that our marketing colleagues John and Ashley are leading needs an additional $5,000 and two more members to be completed by the end of the month. I believe two of us should volunteer to help, since meeting the deadline is important to maintaining a good relationship with our client."

6. Train People to Have Win-Win Interactions

I often ask students to work in pairs to think through how to divide an orange. Each partner is told, without the other's knowledge, a reason for wanting the fruit: One needs to make juice, and the other needs the peel for a muffin recipe. If they fail to explore each other's interests, as most pairs do, the partners may end up fighting over the orange. Or they may decide to cut it in half, giving each side an equal if smaller-than-ideal share. Some people even quit when they can't get the whole orange.

When we communicate, we are often too indirect and abstract

Only a few pairs arrive at the optimal solution, in which one person gets the peel, the other gets the juice, and both are satisfied. How did they get there? By investigating each other's needs.

This approach is the key to win-win interactions. In the successful collaborative projects I examined, people were open about their personal interests and how they thought they could contribute to solving the problem. Such transparency allows participants to explore everyone's vision of winning and, ultimately, get more-favorable results.

Many organizations I've studied teach leaders and employees to find win-win solutions through exercises in which each participant has information that others lack—as is true in most real-world collaborations—and all are asked to try to reach the best deal possible for everyone. Afterward, the instructors suggest techniques that could have helped the parties discover one another's interests better—such as asking questions and listening carefully—and produce more-successful deals. Sometimes the conversations are videotaped and shown to participants after they've had the chance to guess how much of the airtime they got in discussions.

By balancing talking (to express your own concerns and needs) with asking questions and letting others know what your understanding of *their* needs is, you can devise solutions that create more value. With a win-win mindset, collaborators are able to find opportunities in differences.

Because the six techniques are mutually supportive and even interdependent, it's ideal for employees to learn and regularly use them all. It's difficult to have win-win interactions if you spend most of your time talking, and it's tough to learn about others' interests if you don't approach interactions with empathy. And conversations won't be productive if you only listen and don't offer your views—a balance is required.

The techniques also create a positive dynamic: Teammates with whom they're practiced start feeling more respected and in turn are more likely to show others respect. And respect, my research shows, fuels enthusiasm, fosters openness to sharing information and learning from one another, and motivates people to embrace new opportunities for working together.

But this dynamic must be set in motion by those in charge. Many leaders—even ones steeped in enlightened management theory—fail to consistently treat others with respect or to do what it takes to earn it from others.

Leaders who are frustrated by a lack of collaboration can start by asking themselves a simple question: What have they done to encourage it today? It is only by regularly owning their own mistakes, listening actively and supportively to people's ideas, and being respectful but direct when challenging others' views and behavior that they can encourage lasting collaboration. By training people to employ the six techniques, leaders can make creative, productive teamwork a way of life.

———————

Francesca Gino is a behavioral scientist and the Tandon Family Professor of Business Administration at Harvard Business School. She is the author of the books *Rebel Talent: Why It Pays to Break the Rules at Work and in Life* and *Sidetracked: Why Our Decisions Get Derailed, and How We Can Stick to the Plan* (Harvard Business Review Press, 2013).

CHAPTER 15

Seven Strategies for Better Group Decision Making

by Torben Emmerling and Duncan Rooders

When you have a tough business problem to solve, you likely bring it to a group. After all, more minds are better than one, right? Not necessarily. Larger pools of knowledge are by no means a guarantee of better outcomes. Because of an overreliance on hierarchy, an instinct to prevent dissent, and a desire to preserve harmony, many groups fall into groupthink.

Misconceived expert opinions can quickly distort a group decision. Individual biases can easily spread

---

Adapted from content posted on hbr.org, September 22, 2020 (product #H05VFP).

across the group and lead to outcomes far outside individual preferences. And most of these processes occur subconsciously.

This doesn't mean that groups shouldn't make decisions together, but you do need to create the right process for doing so. Based on behavioral and decision science research and years of application experience, we have identified seven simple strategies for more effective group decision making.

Keep the group small when you need to make an important decision

Large groups are much more likely to make biased decisions. For example, research shows that groups with seven or more members are more susceptible to confirmation bias.[1] The larger the group, the greater the tendency for its members to research and evaluate information in a way that is consistent with preexisting information and beliefs. By keeping the group to between three and five people, a size that people naturally gravitate toward when interacting, you can reduce these negative effects while still benefiting from multiple perspectives.

Choose a heterogeneous group over a homogeneous one (most of the time)

Various studies have found that groups consisting of individuals with homogeneous opinions and beliefs have a greater tendency toward biased decision making.[2] Teams that have potentially opposing points of view can more effectively counter biases. However, context matters. When trying to complete complex tasks that require diverse skills and perspectives, such as conducting research and designing processes, heterogeneous groups may substantially outperform homogeneous ones. But in repetitive tasks, requiring convergent thinking in structured environments, such as adhering to safety procedures in flying or health care, homogeneous groups often do better. As a leader, you need first to understand the nature of the decision you're asking the group to make before you assemble a suitable team.

Appoint a strategic dissenter (or even two)

One way to counter undesirable groupthink tendencies in teams is to appoint a devil's advocate. This person is tasked with acting as a counterforce to the group's consensus. Research shows that empowering at least one person with the right to challenge the team's decision-making process can lead to significant improvements in decision quality and outcomes.[3] For larger groups with seven or more members, appoint at least two devil's advocates to be sure that a sole strategic dissenter isn't isolated by the rest of the group as a disruptive troublemaker.

Collect opinions independently

The collective knowledge of a group is only an advantage if it's used properly. To get the most out of your team's diverse capabilities, we recommend gathering opinions individually before people share their thoughts within the wider group. You can ask team members to record their ideas independently and anonymously in a shared document, for example. Then ask the group to assess the proposed ideas, again independently and anonymously, without assigning any of the suggestions to particular team members. By following such an iterative process teams can counter biases and resist groupthink. This process also makes sure that perceived seniority, alleged expertise, or hidden agendas don't play a role in what the group decides to do.

Provide a safe space to speak up

If you want people to share opinions and engage in constructive dissent, they need to feel they can speak up without fear of retribution. Actively encourage reflection on and discussion of divergent opinions, doubts, and experiences in a respectful manner. There are three basic elements required to create a safe space and harness a group's diversity most effectively. First, focus feedback on the decision or discussed strategy, not on the individual. Second, express comments as a suggestion, not as a mandate. Third, express feedback in a way that shows you empathize with and appreciate the individuals working toward your joint goal.

Don't overrely on experts

Experts can help groups make more informed decisions. However, blind trust in expert opinions can make a group susceptible to biases and distort the outcome.[4] Research demonstrates that making them part of the decision making can sway the team to adapt their opinions to those of the expert or make overconfident judgments.[5] Therefore, invite experts to provide their opinion on a clearly defined topic, and position them as informed outsiders in relation to the group.

Share collective responsibility

Finally, the outcome of a decision may be influenced by elements as simple as the choice of the group's messenger. We often observe one single individual being responsible for selecting suitable group members, organizing the agenda, and communicating the results. When this is the case, individual biases can easily influence the decision of an entire team. Research shows that such negative tendencies can be effectively counteracted if different roles are assigned to different group members, based on their expertise.[6] Moreover, all members should feel accountable for the group's decision-making process and its final outcome. One way to do that is to ask the team to sign a joint responsibility statement at the outset, leading to a more balanced distribution of power and a more open exchange of ideas.

Of course, following these steps doesn't guarantee a great decision. However, the better the quality of the decision-making process and the interaction between the group members, the greater your chances of reaching a successful outcome.

Torben Emmerling is the founder and managing partner of Affective Advisory and the author of the D.R.I.V.E.® framework for behavioral insights in strategy and public policy. He is a founding member and nonexecutive director on the board of the Global Association of Applied

Behavioural Scientists (GAABS), and a seasoned lecturer, keynote speaker, and author in behavioral science and applied consumer psychology.

Duncan Rooders is the CEO of a single-family office and a strategic adviser to Affective Advisory. He is a former Boeing 747 pilot, a graduate of Harvard Business School's Owner/President Management program, and an experienced consultant to several international organizations in strategic and financial decision making.

NOTES

1. Dieter Frey et al., "Information Seeking Among Individuals and Groups and Possible Consequences for Decision Making in Business and Politics," in *Understanding Group Behavior*, vol. 2, ed. E. H. Witte and J. H. Davis (Hillsdale, NJ: Lawrence Erlbaum, 1996), 211–225.

2. S. Schulz-Hardt et al., "Biased Information Search in Group Decision Making," *Journal of Personality and Social Psychology* 78, no. 4 (2000): 655–669.

3. David M. Schweiger et al., "Group Approaches for Improving Group Decision Making," *Academy of Management Journal* 29, no. 1 (2017).

4. Dilek Önkal et al., "The Relative Influence of Advice from Human Experts and Statistical Methods on Forecast Adjustments," *Journal of Behavioral Decision Making* 22, no. 4 (2009): 390–409.

5. Andreas Mojzisch et al., "Combined Effects of Knowledge About Others' Opinions and Anticipation of Group Discussion on Confirmatory Information Search," *Small Group Research* 39, no. 2 (2008).

6. Cass R. Sunstein and Reid Hastie, "Making Dumb Groups Smarter," *Harvard Business Review*, December 2014, https://hbr.org/2014/12/making-dumb-groups-smarter.

CHAPTER 16

A Good Meeting Needs a Clear Decision-Making Process

by Bob Frisch and Cary Greene

The tension in the room was rising. The group had been at it for hours. In fact, this same team of 12 had been through essentially the same discussion on three previous occasions but still couldn't reach a decision on a critical issue: *Should the organization divest its South American operation or shift to a different strategy?*

Adapted from content posted on hbr.org, March 5, 2019 (product #H04TSP).

They reviewed the pros and cons of both options yet again. Each side paraded its own experts, data, and recommendations. And yet they remained at an impasse.

In our 60+ years of combined experience working with boards and senior executives at organizations ranging from *Fortune* 10 multinationals to German *mittelstand* companies, we've seen leaders give plenty of thought to the data and analysis needed to kick off and carry on these sorts of discussions. But they typically don't consider how they'd like to finish them.

We're not suggesting they should know in advance *what* decision will be made. But they should know *how* a decision will be made if people can't agree.

In situations where everyone in the room reports to a common manager, and that person is present, there's not much of an issue. If the team can't decide, the boss will. But in today's highly matrixed organizations, closure in the absence of consensus can be an enormous challenge. Team members—even an individual executive—may well have multiple reporting lines. Finding a "natural tiebreaker"—whether one person or another group—may involve decisions bumping up two or even three levels, which is an impractical solution in many cases, and one that risks casting an unfavorable light on the group.

When we ask our clients, "What's going to happen at the end of the conversation if the decision isn't obvious? How exactly will it be made?" the answers often include: "Let's see how it goes," "We'll figure it out," or the classic "We'll cross that bridge when we come to it."

We think that's a bad idea. Your team shouldn't try to make an important decision unless everybody understands what's going to happen if its members can't reach an agreement.

So, before a decision-making meeting starts, be crystal clear about *how* the decision will be made. For example, tell the group there will be 90 minutes of discussion and if there is no resolution after that time, the issue will be put to a vote. While this may seem obvious, be sure to consider how the results will be used in the room. Does the verdict rest directly on the vote, or is the vote merely advisory for the accountable executive? Most decision-making models suggest that one person be accountable for making the final call, but if your organization takes a more collaborative approach, you need to clarify what a vote means. If it determines the decision, what is required? A simple majority? A two-thirds vote? Is anyone given veto power?

Also consider what happens if the executive or team with final authority isn't in the room. How should the issue get elevated? Will the vote be enough input? Should majority and minority viewpoints be documented? If so, how?

Once you've outlined a plan, share it with key stakeholders early so they can ask questions or suggest changes. It doesn't have to be complicated. In fact, it should be clear and simple so that everyone understands the process.

Early in his career Tom Wilson, now chairman, president, and CEO of The Allstate Corporation, used to end each major meeting with a simple chart. For each significant decision, there were three boxes: "Yes," "No," and "Defer." Under the latter, there was space to indicate the date to which the issue would be deferred and what additional actions or data were required to move to a "Yes" or "No" at that time. This helped drive clarity and closure and made his meetings more efficient and decisive.

Teams don't need to get stuck spinning around a whirlpool of indecision. Meetings just need to start with everyone crystal clear on how they will end.

Bob Frisch is the founding partner of the Strategic Off-sites Group. He has written four *Harvard Business Review* articles, including "Off-Sites That Work" (June 2006), and his article "When Teams Can't Decide" (November 2008) was included in *HBR's 10 Must Reads on Teams*. A frequent contributor to hbr.org, Bob also wrote the best-selling book *Who's in The Room? How Great Leaders Structure and Manage the Teams Around Them*. He has facilitated off-sites in 19 countries.

Cary Greene is managing partner of the Strategic Off-sites Group, a consultancy focused on designing and facilitating strategy conversations for executive teams and boards. He is coauthor of the *Harvard Business Review* article "Leadership Summits That Work" (March 2015) and over 10 articles for hbr.org, and his writing has been featured in several HBR collections. Cary also coauthored *Simple Sabotage: A Modern Field Manual for Detecting and Rooting Out Everyday Behaviors That Undermine Your Workplace*.

CHAPTER 17

Four Tips for Effective Virtual Collaboration

by Elizabeth Grace Saunders

Team collaboration done right is a powerful force to align a group of individuals to accomplish a common goal in the most effective way possible. But even the best collaborations, filled with smart, capable, and experienced team members, can be a struggle. Done wrong, collaborative projects can feel like a waste of time where individuals spend more time *talking* about doing things than actually getting things done.

Adapted from content posted on hbr.org, October 13, 2020 (product #H05WGP).

Collaboration is especially difficult in our new era of increased remote work. Organic collaboration is almost impossible when you're working at a distance. Catching up on the latest projects and exciting new experiments— or where a project may be struggling—could easily be covered during frequent hallway chats, but those opportunities won't happen in a remote environment unless you're intentional. And collaboration isn't effective when you loosely and sporadically message about initiatives and don't have a structured approach to answering important questions, aligning team members, and driving to the main goal. For team collaboration to work remotely, you and your teammates must be clear and strategic about how you will collaborate.

The logistics of collaboration are not the only obstacle facing team members. Time is also a concern. Many individuals have more than enough tasks and projects on their plate, and their schedules are more disparate than ever, juggling work and personal obligations. How do you get team members to come together to focus their time and attention on your project?

As a time management coach, I know that to be most effective at work, you have to be purposeful about how you invest every precious minute. Here's how to do team collaboration right, even as you're facing remote work-related challenges.

Use Regular Meetings

If you need to brainstorm, set vision, align roles, agree on goals, or do other creative and strategic discussions, a meeting will likely be your most efficient method for getting these activities done. You may be tempted to add a recurring meeting to the calendar, but when you can, try to work these items into existing standing meetings instead, so you're not adding more to people's already overcrowded schedules. For example, you may decide that once a month your regular team meeting takes a more strategic focus instead of a tactical one. Set an agenda in advance and assign someone to facilitate the meeting to keep the group on track and drive decision making. Also, have someone take notes and route them to stakeholders, so you don't have to waste precious time by having another meeting about the same topic in the future.

Share Documents

If you need feedback on material, and it's OK for the communication to be asynchronous, share a document. You can do this through Google Docs, Teams, Slack, or whatever other file-sharing service is approved by your organization.

When you use this method, be sure to set a deadline for review, turn on track changes, and be clear on exactly what you need from the reviewers in the document. Everything should be self-explanatory, so that if your colleague has to look at the document after they've tucked in their kids at night (and therefore can't reach out to a teammate in the moment), no clarification is required. (See the sidebar, "Five Ways to Make Virtual Collaboration a Little Smoother.")

by Michael D. Watkins

Collaboration has become a fact of business life, so what does it take to make it work effectively? Here are a few basic principles for making this happen:

Clarify tasks and processes, not just goals and roles. Simplify the work to the greatest extent possible, ideally so tasks are assigned to subgroups of two or three team members. And make sure that there is clarity about work process, with specifics about who does what and when. Then periodically do after-action reviews to evaluate how things are going and identify process adjustments and training needs.

Agree on a shared language. Cross-cultural teams have magnified communication challenges—especially when members think they are speaking the same language, but actually are not. Take the time to explicitly negotiate agreement on shared interpretations of important words and phrases, for example, "when we say yes, we mean . . ." and "when we say no, we mean . . . ," and post this in the shared workspace.

Create a "virtual watercooler." Teams need clear ways to share information and reinforce social bonds, especially when they don't work together in person. Try starting each meeting with a check-in, having each member take a couple of minutes to discuss what they are doing, what's going well, and what's challenging. Alternatively, enterprise collaboration platforms increasingly are combining shared workspaces with social networking features that can help team members to feel more connected.

Clarify and track commitments. When teams collaborate remotely, there is no easy way to observe engagement and productivity. One useful tool: a "deliverables dashboard" that is visible to all team members on whatever collaborative hub they are using. If you create this, though, take care not to end up practicing virtual micromanagement.

Foster shared leadership. Defining deliverables and tracking commitments push to keep team members focused and productive; shared leadership provides crucial pull. Find ways to involve others in leading the team. Examples include assigning responsibility for special projects, such as identifying and sharing best practices; or getting members to coach others in their areas of expertise; or assigning them as mentors to help on-board new team members; or asking them to run a virtual team-building exercise.

Michael D. Watkins is a cofounder of Genesis Advisers, a professor at IMD Business School, and the author of *The First 90 Days* and *Master Your Next Move* (both by Harvard Business Review Press).

Adapted from "Making Virtual Teams Work: Ten Basic Principles," on hbr.org, June 27, 2013 (product #H00AUL).

Work Side by Side

If you're back in the office—or never left—working side by side may naturally happen. But for some of my coaching clients who work remotely, I've seen a trend toward virtual side-by-side working. On a video call with a colleague, you do your work on a particular shared project at the same time. This way, you can easily stop and ask them a question or ask for feedback whenever you get stuck. Since the person is already working on something similar, the collaboration can move forward more smoothly. This strategy is also effective if you find yourself avoiding something difficult at work. The positive peer pressure that someone is physically present with you and expects you to get a certain activity done in that window of time can be a good incentive to help you overcome approach avoidance.

Message Away

Although collaborative chat tools, like Slack, Teams, and Flock, are incredibly popular and often seen as the key to team collaboration, make sure that they're working for you instead of you working for them. Decide how often and for how long you'll engage with the appropriate channels. For some of my coaching clients, that can mean as little as 10 minutes once a day to skim through the most relevant messages. For others, it's checking in multiple times a day or having their messaging tool open except for when they need to be super-focused. And if you find that you can't easily solve a problem through chat, switch the conversation to a call. By doing this, you take more control over your time, and the entire team has a better understanding of when they'll hear back from you.

The purpose behind team collaboration isn't for you to always be available. Instead, it's to make sure that you and your team are aligned on your goals and most effectively moving ahead in accomplishing them. You can collaborate effectively when far apart, even when you have an incredible amount to do, if you collaborate with intention and focus.

———————

Elizabeth Grace Saunders is a time management coach and the founder of Real Life E Time Coaching & Speaking. She is author of *How to Invest Your Time Like Money* and *Divine Time Management*. Find out more at www.RealLifeE.com.

CHAPTER 18

If Your Team Agrees on Everything, Working Together Is Pointless

by Liane Davey

Collaboration is crumpling under the weight of our expectations. What should be a messy back-and-forth process far too often falls victim to our desire to keep things harmonious and efficient. Collaboration's promise of greater innovation and better risk mitigation can go

---

Adapted from content posted on hbr.org, January 31, 2017 (product #H03FAC).

unfulfilled because of cultural norms that say everyone should be in agreement, be supportive, and smile all the time. The common version of collaboration is desperately in need of a little more conflict.

You've probably been taught to see collaboration and conflict as opposites. In some cultures, the language and imagery of teamwork is ridiculously idyllic: rowers in perfect sync, or planes flying in tight formation. As a team, you're "all in the same boat." To be a good team player, you must "row in the same direction." These idealized versions of teamwork and collaboration are making many teams impotent.

There's no point in collaboration without tension, disagreement, or conflict. What we need is collaboration where tension, disagreement, and conflict improve the value of the ideas, expose the risks inherent in the plan, and lead to enhanced trust among the participants.

It's time to change your mindset about conflict. Let go of the idea that all conflict is destructive and embrace the idea that productive conflict creates value. If you think beyond the trite clichés, it's obvious: Collaborating is unnecessary if you agree on everything. Building on one another's ideas only gets you incremental thinking. If you avoid disagreeing, you leave faulty assumptions unexposed. As famed writer, reporter, political commentator Walter Lippmann said in his book *The Stakes of Diplomacy*, "Where all think alike, no one thinks very much." To maximize the benefit of collaborating, you need to diverge before you converge.

Unfortunately, our distaste for conflict is so entrenched that encouraging even modest disagreement takes significant effort. I find that three specific techniques help people embrace productive conflict. Carve out some team development time to do these exercises before your next contentious discussion.

Discuss what each team member wants from the conversation

Highlight how the roles are there to drive different agendas. As an example, if you are in a cross-functional meeting with sales and production, the production person might be advocating for more standardization, control, and efficiency. The salesperson advocates for the exact opposite: more flexibility, customization, and agility. When they are doing their jobs well, the sales and production leads should conflict with one another on the path to an optimized solution. One is fighting to be as responsive as possible to unique customer needs; the other fights for the consistency that breeds quality control and cost effectiveness.

As you work through each role in the team and their different motives, you'll see the light bulbs going on as people realize, "You mean I'm *supposed* to fight with that person!" Yes! "And when he's disagreeing with me, it's not because he's a jerk or trying to annoy me?" Right! If the team has the right composition, each member will be fighting for something unique. They are doing their jobs (and being good team players) by advocating in different directions, not by acquiescing. By taking the time to normalize the tensions that collaborators already feel, you liberate them to disagree, push, pull, and fight hard for the best answer.

Highlight differences in what people pay attention to

In addition to differences stemming from their roles, team members will have different perspectives on an issue based on their personalities. As you explore the findings for your team, look for any tensions that might stem from personality-based diversity. Pay particular attention if you have one or two styles that are in the minority on your team. Team members with minority perspectives should be given the responsibility to speak up if the team's thinking becomes lopsided.

For example, in my work with dozens of executive teams, I've found a dearth of executives who fully appreciate the process-related issues involved in strategy and execution. I call out those who have this lens and set the expectation that they are going to challenge the team when big ideas are insufficiently thought out or when alignment is only superficial. By describing the unique value of different perspectives, you encourage those in the minority to raise their voices.

Set ground rules around dissension

Ask your team to define the behaviors that contribute to productive conflict (that is, conflict that improves decision making while contributing to increased trust) and those that detract from it. Cover as much territory as possible to give people a clear picture of what is, and is not, acceptable behavior on your team.

In addition to clarifying appropriate conflict behaviors, you might want to define processes or roles that will help you to have more-frequent or more-effective conflict. Some teams have success with DeBono's Six Thinking Hats, which has team members use a specified perspective (for example, a white hat is logical and fact-based; a black hat is cautious and conservative; a green hat is creative and provocative) to shed new light on the issue at hand. Others assign the responsibility for eliciting diverging views to a rotating chairperson or the owner of the agenda item. Still others use a devil's advocate to question the veracity of evidence and to propose alternate explanations for what has happened. The key is to clearly define the process you're using and the associated expectations.

Even after using these three techniques to change people's mindset about conflict, you have to go further. Giving people permission to challenge, disagree, and argue isn't enough. After all, giving someone permission to do something they don't want to do is no guarantee that they'll do it. If you want to create productive conflict on your team and use it to generate better ideas, you need to move beyond permission to making productive conflict an obligation. Using these three techniques will be a good start.

Liane Davey is a team effectiveness adviser and professional speaker. She is the author of *The Good Fight, You First*, and coauthor of *Leadership Solutions*.

Navigating Conflicts and Power Struggles

How to Permanently Resolve Cross-Department Rivalries

by Ron Carucci

It can be challenging to synchronize complex tasks across multiple functions. Rather than cooperating, too many functions end up competing for power, influence, and limited resources. And such rivalry is more than a nuisance: It's costly. One study reports that 85% of

---

Adapted from content posted on hbr.org, September 25, 2018 (product #H04JWE).

workers experience some regular form of conflict, with U.S. workers averaging 2.8 hours per week.[1] That equates to $359 billion paid hours mired in conflict. It's easy to blame these conflicts on personalities—think toxic bosses or big egos—but in my experience as an organizational consultant, the root cause is more often systemic. For example, this study examining the rivalry between sales and marketing showed that conflicts between managers from these historically warring functions were not driven by interpersonal issues.[2] They were tied to the frequency of how they exchanged information, and the degree to which there were effective processes connecting their work.

When cross-departmental rivalries get heated and conflicts arise, I've frequently seen companies turn to team-building events or motivational speakers who talk about trust. But often the solutions aren't able to address the challenges the groups face because the organizational structure is *encouraging* these departments to dislike and distrust one another. For example, I worked with a global consumer products company in which the commercial organization—the set of departments responsible for developing new products and bringing them to market—was deeply fragmented. There were misunderstandings across the group about what one another did and sharp differences in how each subgroup defined a successfully commercialized product. R&D viewed operations as "the people who only know how to say no to opportunities," while operations viewed R&D as "the time- and money-wasters."

To better integrate and align rivaling functions, and therefore reduce friction and strengthen collaboration, leaders can address four critical questions that enable cross-functional teams to work together more coherently. These can happen over an extended working session, or a series of conversations.

What value do we create together?

The seams that connect major functions are where a company's greatest competitive distinctions lie. Discrete technical capabilities reside within functions, but when blended with the capabilities of adjacent functions, they combine into capabilities that drive performance. But that value is only realized when those functions understand their shared contributions for creating it. In my client example, the people in R&D and operations came to see one another differently, and work more collaboratively, because they realized that their combined expertise was necessary to get products to market faster. Neither alone controlled speed to market, but together they could significantly influence it. R&D needed to be disciplined in how it provided product specifications to manufacturing, and operations needed to be adaptable in order to accommodate new products it had never had to make before. Marketing and R&D's combined value could be creating innovations that prioritize the customer. By identifying which objectives in the organization's strategy the functions mutually contribute to, they reduce the perception of conflicting goals. They also better manage the healthy, natural tensions between objectives like containing cost and investing in opportunities that may not materialize.

What capabilities do we need to deliver the value?

Having anchored their relationship in creating value for the company together, groups can now focus on how best to achieve it. Functions should identify the four to five critical shared capabilities they must have. These may include the translation of market analytics into product opportunities, technical problem-solving, or the fast and accurate exchange of information and learning as projects move through the development process. Identifying these requires an honest assessment of the organization to uncover any lagging or missing capabilities or processes that best integrate each function's efforts. In the case of my client, we discovered there was no forum to bring together all of the commercial functions—regulatory, packaging, manufacturing, and marketing—to discuss potential problems with ongoing projects. As a result, information was slow to get to decision makers, and was often distorted by the time it did. The organization created a monthly meeting for these groups to come together to discuss challenges and solve problems with greater candor.

How will we resolve conflicts and make decisions while maintaining trust?

Conflicts will inevitably come up when trying to better coordinate efforts. Answering this question together presents an opportunity to "rehearse" those conflicts in advance. Functions should identify the critical decisions they'll need to make in pursuit of their cocreated value and determine who gets to make the final call on those decisions. This requires acknowledging any historical baggage or unresolved distrust between the functions. Only when those concerns are fully aired can any biases people have toward one another's department be removed. Empathy is key here, as is sharing information on what it's like to interact with one another. I've often heard people express during this part of the conversation sentiments like, "I had no idea you guys had to do that! No wonder our requests drive you crazy!" The goal is to increase the respect the departments have for one another and build greater commitment to collective success.

What do we need from each other to succeed?

This final question is about supporting one another's work going forward. Groups must create detailed service-level agreements to one another, and negotiate things like timeliness of information sharing, quality standards, how far in advance notification is needed for changes, and how day-to-day work will be coordinated. The departments may need to share access to particular technology platforms or include people from other groups in certain meetings, so they get the information they need and provide input at the right time. Once the group agrees on which commitments they need to make, they must stick to them.

Organizations naturally fragment as they grow, pulling people apart into silos and creating functional borders that can set rivalry in motion. If you see fraying cross-functional relationships, don't resort to superficial solutions like team building or conflict training. Dig deeper to understand what's really causing those fractures and take steps together to set up your functions for mutual success.

———————

Ron Carucci is cofounder and managing partner at Navalent, working with CEOs and executives pursuing transformational change for their organizations, leaders, and industries. He is the bestselling author of eight books, including *To Be Honest: Lead with the Power of Truth, Justice, and Purpose.*

NOTES

1. "Workplace Conflict and How Businesses Can Harness it to Thrive," CPP Global Human Capital Report, July 2008. https://shop.themyersbriggs.com/Pdfs/CPP_Global_Human_Capital_Report_Workplace_Conflict.pdf.

2. Philip L. Dawes and Graham R. Massey, "Antecedents of Conflict in Marketing's Cross-Functional Relationship with Sales," *European Journal of Marketing*, November 1, 2005.

CHAPTER 20

Navigating a Turf War at Work

by Amy Gallo

You're working on a cross-functional initiative that's critical to your company. Given your position, you've assumed you're in charge, but it seems your counterpart from another team has made the same assumption. And now you're in the middle of a turf war. How do you determine who has authority? How do you navigate the situation with your boss, your counterpart, and others in the group? And even if you can come to an agreement, how do you make sure it lasts?

Adapted from "How to Navigate a Turf War at Work," on hbr.org, September 27, 2017 (product #H03X0F).

What the Experts Say

There are lots of reasons that turf wars can happen, says Jeanne M. Brett, professor of dispute resolution and negotiations at Northwestern University's Kellogg School of Management. "Organizations evolve and change, and sometimes people end up doing what your group is already doing." It may also be an intentional power grab. Either way, "these situations can easily become toxic," Brett warns, because they involve egos, emotions, and people's sense of identity. If you're annoyed at your colleague's desire to call the shots, she's highly likely to feel the same way about you, adds Brian Uzzi, professor of leadership and organizational change at Kellogg and coauthor of the HBR article "Make Your Enemies Your Allies." "Research shows that taking something away from someone is experienced as far more harmful than putting an additional burden on them," he explains.[1] But you don't need to start, or continue, the battle. To navigate the situation thoughtfully, follow these principles.

Check your mindset

Though you may feel frustrated, threatened, even angered by the situation, Brett's research shows that "anger doesn't always work" in negotiations like these.[2] Instead, you should go in with "an attitude of innovation"—how can everyone take something satisfying away? "It shouldn't be that you win and they lose, or the other way around. You may be able to expand the pie." Uzzi, too, advocates taking a softer approach, even if you were previously raging inside: You should try to project, "I'm open-minded. I'm a team player. We all want what's best for the organization." And you need to be patient. "You shouldn't have it fixed in your mind that this is going to be resolved in one meeting. You'll likely need a series of meetings to discuss what the issue is, mull the options, propose resolutions, and eventually choose one," Uzzi says.

Focus on the larger goal

Even if you and your peer are vying for the same leadership position or project, you don't have to be mortal enemies. And chances are the person isn't out to get you. "People often don't want to take away control or power— they just want to introduce a new idea" or have more influence, Uzzi says. They may not even realize they're stepping into your territory. "Sometimes people are just doing their jobs, and to do them they end up doing something that's another person's responsibility," Brett says. Rather than focusing on the negative dynamic between you two, think about what your common goal is. "Perhaps it's to do what's best for the organization or to keep strong relationships with your customers or clients," Uzzi says. Concentrating on the higher objective will keep you out of the morass of personal jabs.

Do your research

It may be possible that one of you is actually supposed to be in charge and the other person doesn't know it. Before you take your colleague to task for stepping on your toes, do some research. Ask your boss for clarity or ask other people on the team if they know about a decision that's been made that you weren't privy to. Lack of clarity or even misunderstanding is often at the root of these disputes, Uzzi says. "Perhaps the boss hasn't given you direction. The new project doesn't clearly fall into your team's purview or the other's," he says. Brett agrees: "It's not always crystal clear what should be your responsibility and what should be someone else's."

Problem-solve with your counterpart

If your research doesn't turn up a definitive answer, or you're not happy with it, you can schedule a time to meet with your rival and discuss how to disentangle the roles and responsibilities. You might say: "I'd like to sit down with you to talk about this situation face-to-face." If you think that wouldn't work for them, suggest having someone they respect join the conversation.

Brett points out that while this direct approach is appropriate in most Western cultures, in other areas of the world, such as East Asia, you might want to go to the boss instead: "In a hierarchical culture, that's the boss's job. The manager makes the decision and neither one of you will lose face." In other cultures, you might send someone to ask, "Would you sit down with Sabine to discuss this?" Figure out what's acceptable and go to the appropriate person to start a conversation.

Negotiate the process

Once you're talking to your counterpart, don't dive right into the issues ("Here's why I should be in charge on this"). Brett says it's a better idea to negotiate the process first. You might agree on how long you're going to talk ("Should we spend the next 45 minutes discussing the project and how to move it forward?") or what criteria you'll use to solve the problem. The advantage of doing this is that you tackle a smaller problem before moving on to the meatier issues. "It sets a precedent that you can work together," Brett says. You can also revert to talking about process if your conversation hits a wall. You might say, "We've been talking for 30 minutes and we can't agree on how we got here or what we're going to do about it. Let's step back and see if we can approach it in a different way."

Control your emotions

It's important to remain calm throughout the discussion. These disputes can feel personal ("Does this person think I'm not up to the task of leading the project?"), but you're unlikely to get to a resolution if you yell or act irrational. "If you do start to lose it, be honest about it," Brett recommends. "Say, 'I thought I could talk about this calmly, but I'm struggling with it. Can we set up a different meeting with so-and-so sitting in?'" Of course, you can't control how the other person will behave. But if they start to get hot under the collar, don't react. Let them vent. Brett says you should picture their angry words coming out of their mouth and going right over your shoulder.

Escalate carefully

If you do decide to involve one or both of your managers, or another third party, proceed carefully. By outsourcing the decision to someone else, you "lose control over the outcome," Brett says. And you don't want the higher-ups to think you can't solve your own problems. Brett advises approaching both of your bosses together and saying something like, "We see pros and cons to one of us or the other taking over the project, but we believe the decision needs input from you, as the broader company perspective." Make sure to "frame it as looking out for the interests of the larger organization" rather than as needing a referee for your personal squabble. Keep in mind that some managers may not know how to handle the situation. "The more work experience the boss has, the more likely the person is to act as a mediator," Brett says.

Decide if it's worth it

If your managers are unwilling or unable to help, and you're still at a stalemate, you have to decide whether continuing to fight this battle is worth it. Ultimately, what's best for the organization may not be the same as what's best for your career. For example, a prolonged turf war is likely to damage your relationship with your counterpart, their group, and possibly your broader reputation. At the same time, you need to make sure that bowing out won't cause your team to lose resources or credibility, Uzzi says. Carefully weigh the pros and cons of demanding the leadership role, or gracefully ceding it to your counterpart.

Case Study #1: Ask for Clarity

Crystal Oakman, a program manager in the IT department of a large production company, started working on an enterprise-wide project a few months ago. The project sponsor asked her to lead the effort. "It was an IT software that the entire enterprise uses daily, and so thousands of users were affected. There was a lot of scrutiny by executives," she explains.

The team had a kickoff call, and Crystal thought it was clear that she'd been given the authority to lead the team. But she didn't know that, in a previous discussion, a colleague had been given the same authority and was busy developing a plan to roll out the software.

When she tried to push the project forward, she noticed that this colleague seemed to think he was in charge as well, which stymied progress. "I kept meeting resistance," she recalls. "I can't tell you the [number] of heated moments where he and I were having conversations that were clearly not in line, but neither of us knew it because we both thought we were leading."

The issue wasn't just who was in charge, but how to carry out the project. "I strongly disagreed with some of his strategies," Crystal says. "When I requested that he include other strategies . . . he adamantly disagreed. In my head, I was ultimately responsible for the success of the project, and so I held my ground." They spent hours on the phone debating, and neither would concede.

Crystal tried to send out an org chart that made clear who was in charge, but when she ran it by the project sponsor, he discouraged her from sharing it, saying that it would upset the other program manager to see he was reporting to her. "It was then that I realized my manager had wanted me to 'ghost lead' without leading, leaving another high-level team member on the project with all the authority and decision making."

Crystal wasn't happy with this arrangement, so she told the project sponsor that the effort was going to fail unless they had clearer role descriptions. At that point, she says, "there was no escaping the reality of what was in place." She finally understood the difference between the role she was going to play and the one she had been "sold," so she decided to slowly step back from the work, knowing that it wasn't good for the project—or her—to keep fighting.

Case Study #2: Decide How Far to Push

Joyeeta Das, the CEO and founder of Gyana, a big-data company based in the UK, used to work at a large technology company. During her six years there, she found herself in many situations where it wasn't clear if she was in charge of a project or someone else was. "The best way I could deal with [these situations] was by being candid with both my boss and my colleague," she says.

In one situation, she and another manager were working on highly technical software. When it became clear to her that her colleague thought he was in charge, Joyeeta took her boss out to coffee to casually discuss the situation. She left with some "general tips" on how to handle it, but her manager said, "he didn't want to step in and solve things."

Her next step was to take her colleague out for a similar chat. She conveyed her respect and explained that she was confused about the roles. But he got "upset very quickly," she recalls. He didn't seem to acknowledge her authority or understand her point of view, and she could tell that this conversation had made things worse. So she decided to cede control.

But there were other times when she held her ground, especially when she had data to back her up and she knew that other people in the organization would support her. Knowing when to speak out and when to step out "eventually won me a lot of respect," she says.

Amy Gallo is a contributing editor at *Harvard Business Review* and the author of the *HBR Guide to Dealing with Conflict at Work*. She writes and speaks about workplace dynamics.

NOTES

1. Daniel Kahneman and Amos Tversky, "The Psychology of Preferences," *Scientific American* 246, no. 1 (1982): 160–173.

2. Hajo Adam and Jeanne M. Brett, "Context Matters: The Social Effects of Anger in Cooperative, Balanced, and Competitive Negotiation Situations," *Journal of Experimental Social Psychology* 61 (2015): 44–58.

CHAPTER 21

How to Handle a Disagreement on Your Team

by Jeanne Brett and Stephen B. Goldberg

When you're leading a collaborative project, you can't always ensure that everyone will get along. Given competing interests, needs, and agendas, you might even have two people who vehemently disagree. What's your role as the boss in a situation like this? Should you get involved or leave them to solve their own problems?

Ideally, you'll be able to coach your colleagues to talk to each other and resolve their conflict without involving you, making clear that their disagreement is harmful

---

Adapted from content posted on hbr.org, July 10, 2017 (product #H03RNN).

to them and the organization. But that's not always possible. In these situations, we believe it's important to intervene, not as a boss but as a mediator. To be sure, you won't be a neutral, independent mediator since you have some stake in the outcome, but you're likely to be more effective in meeting everybody's interests—yours, theirs, and the organization's—if you use your mediation skills rather than your authority.

Why rely on mediation and not your authority?

Your colleagues are more likely to own the decision and follow through with it if they're involved in making it. If you dictate what they should do, they will have learned nothing about resolving conflict themselves. Rather, they will have become more dependent on you to figure out their disputes for them. Plus, you might not even have the formal authority to intervene.

Of course, there will be times when you'll have to put aside your mediator role and decide how the conflict will be resolved—for example, if major departmental or company policy issues are involved, there is imminent danger, or all other avenues have failed to resolve the conflict, but those occasions are few and far between.

What if your colleagues expect you to step in as the leader?

Your first move is to recognize your authority, but explain the mediation process you have in mind. You might tell your colleagues that although you have the authority to impose an outcome on them, you hope that, together, you can find a resolution that works for everyone. You could also tell them that when the three of you are to-gether, they should devote their energy to reaching agreement, rather than trying to persuade you which of their views should prevail.

Should you initially meet with each colleague separately or jointly?

There are pros and cons to both approaches. The goal is to understand both of their positions (what one is claim-ing and the other rejecting) and their interests (why they are making and rejecting the claims).

Conflict often carries with it a heavy dose of emotion. One or both of your colleagues may be seriously angry. One or both may feel intimidated by the other. Meeting with each separately will give the angry colleague an op-portunity to vent, give you a chance to reassure the in-timidated colleague that you will listen, and may surface information ultimately useful to resolving the conflict—information that colleagues either haven't shared with each other or haven't heard if shared.

If you first sit down with them separately, don't focus the discussion on how to resolve the conflict, but rather on gaining an understanding of the disagreement and convincing each that you are willing to listen and anx-ious to understand their concerns.

Research has shown that initial separate meetings are more successful if the manager spends time build-ing empathy and gaining an understanding of the problem.[1] There will be plenty of time in subsequent meetings to talk about how to resolve the conflict. Also be sure in this initial meeting that you are using empathy ("That must have been really hard for you") and not sympathy ("I feel sorry for what you have been through"). An expression of empathy is respectful but relatively neutral, and it does not imply support for the person's position.

The risk in starting separately is that each colleague may think that the other is going to use that meeting to sway you to the other's perspective. You can avoid this by explaining that the purpose of the meeting is to understand both sides of what is going on, not for you to form an opinion on who is right and who is wrong.

Meeting jointly at first has its upsides, too. Giving each a chance to do some controlled venting in a joint session may clear the air between them. You should check with both before proposing this approach since you want to be sure that they can engage in such a session without losing their composure, making resolution even more difficult. And be sure to set some ground rules—each will have a turn, without interruptions, for example—before you begin and be prepared to tightly control the session and even break it off if you cannot control it; otherwise it can turn brutal.

Another good reason to have your colleagues meet together is that ultimately, they need to own the resolution of their conflict and they need to develop the ability to talk to each other when future conflicts arise. Of course, the risk in meeting jointly is that you cannot control the process and the meeting only escalates the conflict.

Keep in mind that you don't have to pick one mode of meeting and stick with it throughout the process. You can switch between modes. However, our research suggests that starting separately and building empathy and then moving to a joint meeting is more effective in resolving conflict than starting jointly and then meeting separately.[2]

What should you accomplish in your first meeting?

Whether you're meeting together or not, there are several things you want to do in the initial meeting. Explain that you see your role as helping them find a mutually acceptable resolution to their conflict, but also ensuring that the resolution does not have negative implications for the team or the organization. Make clear that deciding whether a particular agreement is acceptable requires their buy-in and yours. And then set out some rules for whenever you meet together. For example, treat each with respect and don't interrupt.

The goal of the initial meeting is to have them leave with emotions abated and feeling respected by you, if not yet by each other. With that done, you can then bring them together (if you didn't meet jointly the first time) and focus on getting the information that you all need in order to resolve the conflict.

What information do you need to draw out in subsequent meetings?

In order to resolve the conflict, you'll need to know from both people their positions (what each wants), interests (why each is taking that position, how the position reflects their needs and concerns), and priorities (what is more and less important to each and why).

You can gather this information by doing several things: asking "why?" or "why not?" questions to uncover the interests that underlie their positions, listening carefully to identify those interests, reformulating what you think you understand about one colleague's interests to make sure you understand and that the other colleague also is hearing them.

What are the pitfalls to avoid?

There are several ways that these discussions can go wrong. For one, either colleague can try to convince you that their view of the facts is the only correct view, that their position is the "right" one, or that they should prevail because they have more power. We call these facts, rights, and power arguments, and they are detrimental because they distract everyone from seeking a resolution that will satisfy everyone's interests.

The facts argument is an interesting one. Both colleagues may have been at the same scene, but each remembers it differently. They both think that if they could only convince you and their colleague of their view of the facts, the conflict would be over. The problem is that even if you had been there, it is counterproductive to try to convince others of your view, because without new credible information they are unlikely to change their minds about what happened. The best approach to closing this trap is to agree to disagree and move on.

Arguments about rights may come in the form of appeals to fairness or past practices. The problem is that for every rights argument one colleague makes, the other can make a different one, which supports their own position. What one party views as fair, the other views as unfair and vice versa. If they start to invoke fairness, suggest that the discussion be put aside temporarily, while you jointly search for information that might be useful in resolving the conflict.

Power arguments are basically threats: "If you don't agree to my position, I will . . ." Being threatened makes people defensive and distrustful, which makes them more reluctant to share information about positions, interests, and priorities. If one person issues a threat, explicit or implicit, remind your colleagues of the ground rules of respect. You might also repeat what you are trying to do—share relevant information to get to a resolution—and that discussion of what one will do if there is no settlement is counterproductive at this point.

How can you move forward toward an agreement?

Finding potential settlements may be easy if, in the process of helping your colleagues understand their different positions and interests, it becomes clear that this conflict was just a misunderstanding or that there is a way forward that respects both parties' interests. If it becomes apparent that their interests are as much in conflict as their positions, finding a settlement may be more difficult, but don't give up.

Our research shows there are several ways to facilitate an agreement in this situation. Surprisingly often, parties can simply agree on how they are going to interact or address the issues in the future. They put the past behind them, accepting that past practice wasn't working for one or the other or both and move forward together. This can be tricky though. Sometimes one might be willing to engage in a future-based agreement like this but not trust the other to follow through on it. In those cases, where uncertainty is a concern, you can try one of these types of agreements:

- **Limited duration.** Agreements that last for a limited time and then are evaluated before continuing.

- **Contingent.** Agreements that depend on a future event *not* happening. If the future event does happen, an alternative agreement takes effect.

- **Non-precedent setting.** Agreements that protect against risk by parties agreeing that the settlement will not set a precedent in the event a similar conflict arises in the future.

It's best if your colleagues can propose resolutions that meet their own and the other's interests. You may be able to coach them into making such proposals by summarizing the interests and priorities as you've heard them. Meeting separately to encourage candor, you might ask each colleague to make a proposal that takes into account the interests and priorities of the other. Discourage each from making unrealistic proposals that would offend the other. You might warn them not to make an offer they cannot reasonably justify, because doing so will compromise their credibility.

If, despite everyone's efforts, you can't reach an agreement, you might need to speak with each colleague separately about the consequences of not reaching a resolution. You can ask, "What do you think will happen if you don't reach agreement?" The answer, of course, is they don't know. The only way to control the outcome of the conflict is if they resolve it themselves.

If there is still no settlement at this point, you may need to shed your mediator role and, as the leader, impose an outcome that is in the best interests of the organization. Be sure to explain your reasoning and make clear this isn't your desired path. You might also point out that your goal in having them work hard in resolving the dispute on their own is so that they are better equipped to do so in the future, and that goal hasn't been fully accomplished. But don't let them walk away thinking their relationship is doomed. Give them both feedback on what they might do differently next time, making clear that when they butt heads again, you'll expect them to manage it on their own.

Jeanne Brett is DeWitt W. Buchanan, Jr. Professor Emerita at the Kellogg School of Management at Northwestern University. She is the author of *Negotiating Globally*.

Stephen B. Goldberg is a professor of law emeritus at Northwestern Pritzker School of Law, where he taught negotiation, mediation, and arbitration. He is also an experienced mediator and arbitrator.

Professors Brett and Goldberg, together with William L. Ury, are the authors of *Getting Disputes Resolved: Designing Systems to Cut the Costs of Conflict*.

NOTES

1. Roderick I. Swaab and Jeanne M. Brett, "Caucus with Care: The Impact of Pre-Mediation Caucuses on Conflict Resolution," IACM 2007 Meetings Paper, January 6, 2008, https://papers.ssrn.com/sol3/papers.cfm?abstract_id=1080622.

2. Stephen B. Goldberg et al., *How Mediation Works* (Bingley, UK: Emerald Publishing Limited, 2017).

CHAPTER 22

Collaborating with People You Don't Like

by Mark D. Nevins

A few months ago, a former client—let's call her Kacie—called me to check in. I had supported her through her transition when she had joined a prestigious global financial services firm several months prior. Given how deliberately and thoughtfully she'd gone through the process, I expected that our conversation would be about her early wins.

Instead, Kacie confessed that she had a simple but serious problem: She wasn't getting along well with a peer—let's call her Marta. The two had gotten off on the

Adapted from content posted on hbr.org, December 4, 2018 (product #H04OHH).

wrong foot, and as time passed, things weren't getting any better. Kacie told me that it was becoming painfully clear that her inability to get along with Marta was going to impede her success and possibly derail her career at the company.

As Kacie and I explored the situation, she told me that Marta was seen as a highly talented, accomplished, and well-liked executive—she wasn't toxic or difficult. But Kacie admitted that she didn't really *like* Marta. They had different styles, and Marta rubbed her the wrong way.

Over a series of conversations, Kacie and I worked through the situation. A few weeks prior, she had mapped out the stakeholders who were important to her role, which clearly showed that Marta's collaboration and partnership were essential for getting the business results Kacie wanted. In assessing the relationship more honestly, Kacie came to realize that she had been failing to reach out to Marta. She had not made her new colleague feel as if her input and perspectives were valuable, had been leaving her and her team off communications, and had more or less been trying to avoid her.

Kacie and I developed a handful of useful strategies for working better with Marta. While none were particularly easy or comfortable, these are ideas and insights that almost anyone can use when they have to work with someone they just don't like.

Reflect on the cause of tension and how you are responding to it

The first step is acceptance and reflection. Remind yourself: You won't get along with everyone, but there is potential value in every interaction with others. You can and should learn from everyone you meet, and the responsibility for making that happen lies with you—even if the relationship is not an easy one. Take an honest look at what is causing the tension and what role you are playing in creating it. Your own reaction to the situation may be at the core of the problem (and you can't control anything other than your reaction). Kacie had to recognize that Marta's "unlikability" may really have been about Kacie herself.

Work harder to understand the other person's perspective

Few people get out of bed in the morning with the goal of making your life miserable. Make time to think deliberately about the other person's point of view, especially if that person is essential to your success. Ask yourself: Why are they acting this way? What might be motivating them? How do they see me? What might they want and need from me? Kacie began to think differently about Marta when she realized that her colleague had goals and motivations as valid as her own and that their goals were not inherently in conflict.

Become a problem solver rather than a critic or competitor

To work better together, it's important to shift from a competitive stance to a collaborative one. One tactic is to "give" the other person the problem. Rather than trying to work through or around the other person, engage them directly. Kacie invited Marta out to lunch and was open with her: "I don't feel as if we are working together as effectively as we could. What do you think? Do you have any ideas for how we can work better together?" If you ask people to show you their cards, and demonstrate vulnerability in the process, they will often reveal a few of their own.

Ask more questions

In tense situations, many of us try to "tell" our way through it. We might become overly assertive, which usually makes the situation worse. Instead, try asking questions—ideally open-ended ones intended to create conversation. Put aside your own agenda and ask thoughtful questions that will lead to sharing and dialogue. Most important, have the patience to truly listen to the other person's answers. Too often in situations of conflict, we listen to the other person just to find weaknesses we can exploit, which is not productive.

Enhance your awareness of your interpersonal style

It's easy to chalk up conflicts to poor chemistry with another person, but everyone has different styles and often being aware of those differences can help. Over lunch, Marta and Kacie discovered that they had both completed the Myers-Briggs Type Indicator earlier in their careers, so they shared their profiles. Kacie is a clear introvert and a very strong sensing type: She prefers to have time to work through issues alone and quietly, drawing conclusions from a broad base of data. Marta, on the other hand, is an extrovert and a strong intuitive type, comfortable reacting immediately, focusing on the big picture, and solving problems by talking them through with others. Given these differences in style and preference, Kacie and Marta were bound to find interacting with each other uncomfortable. Once they identified their differences, they realized that their styles could be quite complementary if they adapted and accommodated their approaches.

Ask for help

Asking for help can reboot a difficult relationship because it shows that you value the other person's intelligence and experience. Over their lunch, Kacie grew confident enough to say to Marta, "You've been around here longer than I have. I feel as if I'm starting to figure things out, but I'd love your help." Then she asked questions like: "What should I be doing more or less of? Am I missing anything or failing to connect with anyone I really should? What do you wish someone had told you when *you* first started working here?"

Partly due to the changes Kacie made to her style and intent, her relationship with Marta improved significantly. During my last call with Kacie, she told me that she and Marta communicate frequently in person and via text and Slack, and that they regularly take part in each other's team meetings. Furthermore, each quarter they bring their teams together to assess progress and seek opportunities to learn and improve their processes. While Marta and Kacie aren't necessarily friends and don't spend a lot of time together outside the office, they're much better colleagues, and they like each other more than they initially expected.

Kacie's success in turning around her relationship with Marta was in part because she acted "while the cement was still wet." Her negative dynamic with Marta hadn't yet hardened, so Kacie was able to increase her self-awareness, adapt her style, and reach out. It *is* possible to collaborate effectively with people you don't like, but *you* have to take the lead.

Mark D. Nevins, PhD, is the president of Nevins Consulting, advising and coaching CEOs and their teams on leadership, strategy, change, and organization effectiveness. He is a regular *Forbes* contributor and coauthor, with John Hillen, of *What Happens Now: Reinvent Yourself as a Leader Before Your Business Outruns You.*

Index

"A" players 58, 60. *See also* star
    players
accountability, personal, 18, 22–
    23. *See also* responsibility
affirmative assertions, 138
agile teams, 65–76, 111–119
    bridging silos and, 67, 68,
        71–73
    engaging fringe players and,
        67, 68, 70–71
    leveraging boundary spanners
        and, 67, 68, 73–75
    managing the network's center
        and, 67–69
    rightsizing, 112–113
agreements, mediation and,
    213–215
AllianceBernstein (AB), 59
Allstate Corporation, 173–174
American Express, 158
Apple, 56
artifacts, cultural, 92, 93–94
assumptions, 4
    about roles, 87–90
    about star players, 56

conflicting, designing solu-
    tions for, 94–95
self-awareness of, 20
shared, in subcultures, 92, 93
attitudes, 136–137, 148
    turf wars and, 198–199
authority
    influence without, 9–15
    mediation vs. in conflict reso-
        lution, 208–209
    turf wars and, 199–200
autonomy, 81–82, 89–90

BBC, 88–89
behaviors
    burnout and, 27
    giving feedback on, 155–156
    for productive conflict,
        186–187
    subcultures and, 93
    universal needs and, 81–82
beliefs
    burnout and, 27
    self-awareness of, 19–20

Bell, Suzanne (researcher), 44
biases. *See also* perspectives
    cognitive, 101–102
    confirmation, 166
Bird, Alan, 55–64
blame, 83–84
Boeing 777 airliner, 61
boundaries, spanning external,
    73–75
brainstorming, 157
Brett, Jeanne M., 198, 200,
    201–202, 207–216
broaden-and-build mode, 80–81
burnout, avoiding, 25–35, 68–69
Busch, Kyle, 57
business development initia-
    tives, 73
buy-in, 12

Cable, Dan, 50
Caesars Entertainment, 59,
    61–62
capabilities. *See* skills
Carucci, Ron, 191–196
Chamorro-Premuzic, Tomas,
    39–45
change, leading without author-
    ity, 9–15
clarity
    about voting, in decision mak-
        ing, 173–174
    on commitments, 179
    in communication, 160–161
    turf wars and, 199–200,
        203–204
    in virtual collaboration, 178
Clark, Dorie, 47–53
Clooney, George, 63
coaches and coaching, 155,
    157–158

coalition building, 12, 13–14
cognitive biases, 101–102
Cohn, Alisa, 50
collaboration
    multidisciplinary, 71–73
    with people you don't like,
        217–222
    psychological approach to,
        148–163
    sustaining, 147–163
    unequal distribution of,
        68–69
    virtual, 15, 33–34, 175–181
collaboration capital, 48–53
collaborative overload, 25–35
command-and-control leader-
    ship, 10
commitments, clarifying and
    tracking, 179
communication, 2
    about motivation, 130–131,
        134–140
    about rightsizing, 117–118
    anticipating reactions to,
        82–83
    asking for feedback on, 84
    clarity vs. abstractions in,
        160–161
    cross-cultural, 178
    information exchange in,
        102–103, 195, 211–212
    listening in, 149–155
    norms for, 33–34
    shared language and, 178
    in team success, 39–40
    time spent by managers in, 26
    understanding impact of your,
        20–21
    universal needs and, 81–82
    in virtual collaboration, 15,
        180–181

win-win interactions in, 161–162
communities of practice, 73
competition, 219–220
confidence, 80
confirmation bias, 166
conflict
    blame and criticism in, 83–84
    collaborative vs. adversarial approach to, 81
    cross-department, 191–196
    embracing, 184–187
    handling in teams, 207–216
    maintaining trust and, 194–195
    mediation for, 207–216
    with people you don't like, 217–222
    personality and, 44
    turf wars, 197–205
    weighing the costs of, 202, 204–205
Conger, Jay A., 10–15
Connected Commons, 26, 66
consensus, 172–173
consultation, 12
context
    for decision making, 166–167
    motivation and, 132
    for teamwork, 115
contingencies, 98–99
contingent agreements, 214
control
    bridging silos and, 72
    burnout and, 29
    delegating and, 159–160
    emotional, 201
    flexing and, 158
    in mediation, 210–211
    turf wars and, 198–202, 204–205

coordinated work, 114
creativity
    conflict in encouraging, 5, 187
    expanding others' thinking and, 153–154
    meetings and, 176–177
    perceived need for, 88
    psychological safety and, 80
    star players and, 55, 57–58
Crocker, Alia, 65–76
Cross, Rob, 25–35, 65–76
cross-department rivalries, 191–196
cross-functional initiatives, 197–205
culture
    agile teams and, 65, 71
    always-on work, 27
    espoused vs. lived, 92
    of fear, 71
    norms of collaboration and, 183–184
    problem-solving approaches and, 200
    shared language and, 178
    subcultures in teams, 91–95
curiosity, 40–41, 80
    judgment vs., 152–153
    replacing blame with, 83–84

Das, Joyeeta, 204–205
dashboards, deliverables, 179
data analytics, 72–73
Davey, Liane, 183–187
DeBono's Six Thinking Hats, 187
decision making, 5
    agile teams and, 65
    embracing conflict for, 184–187

decision making (*continued*)
  groupthink in, 101–103,
    163–170
  if-then planning and, 101–108
  lost causes and, 104–108
  processes for in meetings,
    171–174
  resolving conflicts and main-
    taining trust in, 194–195
  strategies for better, 163–170
  turf wars and, 201–202
defensiveness, 82
delegation, 159–160
deliverables dashboards, 179
Delizonna, Laura, 79–85
Deresiewicz, William, 20
devil's advocates, 167, 187
differences
  embracing, 1–6
  group decision making and,
    166–167
  importance of, 183–187
  as learning opportunities,
    92–94
  in motivation, 126–129
  overidentification with organi-
    zations and, 104–105
  self-awareness and, 18–22
  in subcultures, 91–95
  in teams, 91–95, 183–187
  understanding vs. resenting, 5
Disney, 57–58
dissent
  constructive, 168
  safe space for, 168
  setting ground rules around,
    186–187
  strategic, 167
diversity. *See* differences
document sharing, 177–179
Dream Team (basketball), 62–63

ecosystems, spanning boundaries
  in, 73–75
ego, 56, 62–63, 149
Emmerling, Torben, 165–170
emotional intelligence, 39–40,
    80–81
emotions
  conflict mediation and,
    209–211
  motivation and, 128
  self-awareness of, 19–20
  stability in, 40–41
  turf wars and, 198–199, 201
empathy, 128, 148
  in conflict mediation, 209–
    211
  conflict resolution and, 195
  listening for the unspoken
    and, 154–155
  training people to practice,
    153–155
engagement, 84–85
environment
  agile teams and, 71
  for lateral leadership, 14–15
  of psychological safety, 79–85
Erickson, Tammy, 87–90
evidence
  countering defensiveness with,
    139
  in motivating others, 139
  on motivating others, 122
  questioning, 187
  in rightsizing teamwork,
    113
execution, overcoming obstacles
  to, 99–101
expectations, 32, 91–92, 130,
    183, 186
expertise
  bridging silos and, 72, 73

finding hidden, 70–71
managing differences and, 3–4
motivating for agile collaboration, 72–73
over-reliance on in decision making, 168–169
team role definition and, 89
when asking someone to collaborate, 49–50

fairness, 212–213
feedback
asking for, 21, 84
in decision making, 168
document sharing for, 177–179
making people comfortable with, 155–158
fight-or-flight response, 80, 81
file-sharing services, 177
financing, asking someone to collaborate and, 51–52
flexibility, 135, 158
Fredrickson, Barbara, 80
Frisch, Bob, 171–174
functional focus, 13–14
functional overhauls, 61–62
functional roles, 41–42
funding, convincing someone to collaborate with you and, 51–52

Gallo, Amy, 197–205
Gardner, Heidi K., 65–76
Gino, Francesca, 147–163
goals. *See also* objectives
creating team, 98–99
if-then planning and, 100–101, 106–108
in mediation, 209–211

motivation and, 122–123
reframing, motivation and, 133–135
subgoals in, 106–108
turf wars and focus on, 199
Goldberg, Stephen B., 207–216
Gollwitzer, Peter, 102–103, 104, 105
Google, 39–40, 79
Gottman, John, 83
Grant, Heidi, 97–109
Greene, Cary, 171–174
groupthink, 101–103, 163–170
Gyana, 204–205

habits, creating, 99–101
handoffs, 113–114
help, asking for, 221–222
"hidden gems" programs, 70–71

identity
accomplishment-based, 28, 29–30
conformity and, 104
perceived attacks on, 82
power struggles and, 198
if-then plans, 98–109
cues in, 99–101
neurology and, 98–99
overcoming obstacles with, 99–101
solving problems with, 101–108
image, asking someone to collaborate with you and, 52–53
incentives, 65. *See also* motivation
for agile collaboration, 72
motivation and, 121

inclusivity, 112–113
influence, 9–15
information exchange, 102–103,
      195, 211–212. *See also*
      communication
initiatives
   business development, 73
   cross-functional, 197–205
   strategic, 67
innovation, attitude of,
      198–199
Institute for Corporate Produc-
      tivity, 69
interdependent work, 114–115
interpretations, self-aware-
      ness of, 19–21. *See also*
      perspectives

Jobs, Steve, 57
Johnson, Lauren Keller, 9–15
"Just Like Me" reflection, 82

Kahneman, Daniel, 104
Kaiser, Robert B., 112–119
Katzenberg, Jeffrey, 57–58
knowing-doing gap, 99

Lancefield, David, 49–50
lateral leadership, 10–15
leaders and leadership
   in conflict mediation,
      208–209
   exerting influence without
      authority, 9–15
   fostering shared, 179
   in giving permission to say no,
      117–118

imposing resolutions and, 215
from the inside out, 153–154
lateral, 10–15
leading *and* following,
      158–160
in managing differences, 2
in motivating experts, 72–73
motivation and, 127–129
personal accountability in, 18,
      22–23
self-awareness for, 17–23
for star teams, 58, 63–64
in sustaining collaboration,
      163
team role definition and, 90
learning mindset, 83–84
Le Bernardin restaurant, 55
leverage questioning, 138–140
limited duration agreements,
      214
Lippmann, Walter, 184
listening, 149–153
   allowing silence in, 152
   asking questions in, 150
   focus on the listener and,
      150–151
   self-checks in, 151–152
   for what isn't being said,
      154–155
Listen Like a Leader, 151–153
losing, hatred of, 81
lost causes, 101–102, 104–108

manipulation, negotiation vs.,
      11–12
Mankins, Michael, 55–64
marketing/sales rivalries, 192,
      193
Mars crew, 41, 44

mediation, 207–216
    meetings for, 209–212
    moving toward agreement in,
        213–215
    pitfalls in, 212–213
    using authority vs., 208–209
meetings, 33
    for conflict mediation,
        209–212
    decision-making processes for,
        171–174
    "Sure, boss," 126, 139
    for virtual collaboration,
        176–177
mentors and mentoring, 14–15,
    71
Microsoft, 56, 59–60
mindset, 83–84, 105
    turf wars and, 198–199
moments of truth, 140
morale, star players and, 63
motivation, 121–143
    blocking and unblocking,
        127–129, 140–141
    creating a rich picture for,
        129–133
    examples of problems with,
        123–125
    of experts for agile collabora-
        tion, 72–73
    mistakes managers make
        around, 125–126
    new approach to, 126–129
    reframing goals and, 133–135
    resolutions vs. solutions for,
        126, 128–129, 140–143
    staging encounters for,
        135–140
    tell and sell approach to,
        125

Musk, Elon, 41
Myers-Briggs Type Indicator,
    220–221

narratives, inner, 19
NASA, 41, 44
NASCAR, 57
negotiation
    in cross-departmental conflict,
        195–196
    for lateral leadership, 11–12
    respect in, 81–82
    of role demands, 69, 88
    in turf wars, 200–201
networks and networking
    agile teams and, 66–69
    bridging silos and, 67, 68,
        71–73
    burnout and, 27, 31–33
    convincing someone to col-
        laborate with you and,
        50–51
    engaging the fringe of, 67, 68,
        70–71
    lateral, 67–69
    for lateral leadership, 11, 13–14
    managing the center of, 67–69
    quality vs. quantity in, 34–35
    spanning external boundaries
        in, 67, 68, 73–75
Nevins, Mark D., 217–222
Nicholson, Nigel, 121–143
non-precedent setting agree-
    ments, 214
norms, 92, 183–184

objectives
    in conflict mediation, 211–212

objectives (*continued*)
  cross-department rivalries
    and, 193–194
  defining the path to, 88
  getting teams to accomplish,
    97–109
  managing differences in, 4
  north star, 31, 32–33
Ocean's Eleven, 63
Olympic Games, Dream Team
  for, 62–63
openness, 148, 163
operations, 193–194
opinions, gathering for decision
  making, 167–168
organizational structure
  agile teams and, 66–67
  cross-department rivalries
    and, 191–196
  turf wars and, 197–205
overload
  avoiding burnout from, 25–35
  knowing why you accept,
    29–31
  surge and slow-burn, 27–29
oxytocin, 81

partnerships, 10, 47–53
performance. *See also* motivation
  assessment methods, 59–60
  dealing with poor, 142–143
  emotional intelligence and,
    39–40
  if-then planning and, 99
  personality and, 40–41
  recognizing "B" players', 63
  of star players, 57
personality
  collaborating with people you
    don't like and, 217–222

highlighting differences in
  perspectives and, 186
motivation and, 129–133
Myers-Briggs Type Indicator,
  220–221
team functioning and, 39–45
perspectives
  conflict mediation and,
    209–211
  highlighting differences in, 186
  managing differences in, 3–4
  motivation and, 129–133
  network fringe players and,
    70–71
  of people you don't like, 219
  recognizing other valid, 19–20
persuasion
  in conflict mediation, 212–213
  getting someone to collaborate
    with you, 47–53
  for lateral leadership, 11–12
Pixar, 57–58, 150, 153–158
planning, if-then, 98–109
Porter, Jennifer, 17–23
power arguments, 213
pragmaticism, 42, 43
problems, anticipating, 62–64
problem solving
  in effective teams, 5
  if-then planning for, 101–108
  imposing answers on others
    and, 12
  managing differences in, 4
  with people you don't like,
    219–222
  personal accountability in, 18,
    22–23
  positive emotion and, 80–81
  psychological safety and, 85
  in turf wars, 200
process and rule followers, 42, 43

processes
    agile teams and, 66–67
    rightsizing teamwork and,
        116, 117
    subcultures and, 93
process knowledge, in asking
        someone to collaborate, 50
product development, 61, 67
productivity
    avoiding burnout and, 33–35
    laying groundwork for lateral
        leadership and, 13–14
    psychological safety and,
        79–85
    of star players, 55–56, 57
    team subcultures and, 91–95
projects, mission-critical, 60–62
promotions, 136–137
prospect theory of psychology,
        81
psychological roles, 41–42
psychological safety, 79–85
    for group decision making,
        168
    measuring, 84–85
Pulakos, Elaine D., 111–119

questions and questioning
    in attentive listening, 150
    balancing in communication,
        161–162
    in effective teams, 4–5
    expansive, 150
    leverage questioning, 138–140
    for people you don't like, 220

R&D, 193–194
reactions, anticipating, 82–83
reflection, 32–33

on people you don't like,
        218–219
    on universal needs, 82
reframing, 133–135, 202
relationships
    across ecosystems, 74
    agile teams and, 66–67
    asking someone to collaborate
        and, 47–53
    building in virtual teams, 15
    convincing someone to col-
        laborate with you and,
        47–53
    focus on, 42–44
    with people you don't like,
        217–222
    positive emotion and, 80–81
    quality vs. quantity in, 34–35
    in virtual collaboration,
        178–179
reporting structures, 66–67
reputation, 29–31, 52–53
respect, 112–113, 148, 163, 211
responsibility
    assigning in virtual collabora-
        tion, 179
    in group decision making, 169
    if-then planning and, 99
    motivation and, 123–124,
        126–129, 131–132
    taking, 18
    turf wars and, 199–200
results orientation, 42, 43
Reuters, 89–90
rights, 212–213
risk management, 69
rivalries, cross-department,
        191–196
Roberts, John (U.S. Supreme
        Court chief justice), 56
role-playing, 160–161

roles
    burnout and, 27, 31–33
    clearly defining, 87–90
    embracing conflict and, 185,
        186–187
    functional and psychological,
        41–44
    for group decision making, 169
    personality and, 40
    rightsizing teamwork and,
        116–117
    understanding employees'
        ability to fill new, 59
Rooders, Duncan, 165–170
Root, James, 55–64

sales/marketing rivalries, 192
Santagata, Paul, 79, 81–95
Saunders, Elizabeth Grace,
    175–181
saying no, 29–31, 117–118
Schramm, Philipp, 151
Schwarz, Roger, 91–95
Scripps Research, 115
self-awareness, 17–23, 137
    external, 20–21
    internal, 18–20
    sustaining collaboration and,
        159
self-presentation, 149
self-worth, 29–30
service-level agreements,
    195–196
silos, bridging, 68, 71–73
simplification strategy, 115–117
Six Thinking Hats, 187
skills, 6. See also expertise
    for lateral leadership, 11–12
    for self-improvement, 19–23
    star players and, 55–64

    teaching collaboration,
        148–163
    for teams, 39–45
    for value delivery, 194
    for your north star objectives,
        32–33
"skill-will model," 160
stack ranking, 59–60
stakeholders, connectivity to key
    external, 74–75
The Stakes of Diplomacy
    (Lippmann), 184
star players, 55–64
strategic dissenters, 167
strategic initiatives, 67
strengths, knowing team, 58–59
subject-matter knowledge, 49–50
success, supporting others',
    195–196
sunk costs, fixation on, 101–102,
    104–108
support, 195–196
"Sure, boss" meetings, 126, 139
sweat equity, 49
synchronized work, 114
synergy, 57–58

talent
    hoarding, 59
    management of, 58–60
    pipeline for, 60
Taylor, Scott, 25–35
teams and teamwork
    accomplishing goals in,
        97–109
    agile, 65–76, 112–119
    anticipating problems in,
        62–64
    challenges of, 111–112
    chemistry in virtual, 15

conflict management in,
207–216
coordinated work in, 114
defining the right kind of,
113–115
disincentives for working
together in, 59–60
embracing conflict in, 184–187
giving permission to say no to,
117–118
handoffs in, 113–114
importance of, 111–112
importance of differences in,
183–187
interdependencies between,
69
interdependent work in,
114–115
for mission-critical projects,
60–62
personal accountability in,
22–23
personalities vs. skills in,
39–45
psychological safety for, 79–85
rightsizing, 112–113, 115–117
role definition for, 87–90
self-awareness and, 17–23
signs of effective, 4–5
simplifying, 115–117
star players in, 55–64
strategy definition for, 116–117
subcultures in, 91–95
synchronized work in, 114
technology, 27
always-on work and, 27
for file sharing, 177
virtual collaboration tools,
33–34
"tell and sell" approach to motivation, 125

Thailand, soccer team rescue
in, 158
thinking
expanding others', 153–154
importance of differences in,
183–187
managing differences in, 3–4
"tell and sell" approach to
motivation and, 125
threats, 213
Thürmer, J. Lukas, 102–103,
104, 105
time
consuming others', 34
for lateral leadership development, 13–14
managing to avoid burnout,
31–33
meetings and, 33
for motivation, 128–129
for reflection, 32–33
spent on communication, 26,
33–34
for virtual collaboration, 176,
180–181
wasted on rivalries, 191–192
Toy Story, 57–58
training
for lateral leadership, 14–15
to lead and follow, 158–160
to practice empathy, 153–155
speaking with clarity in,
160–161
for win-win interactions,
161–162
training techniques, 148–163
on feedback, 155–158
practicing empathy, 153–155
teaching people to listen, not
talk, 149–153
transparency, 161–162

trust, 70–71
  asking for feedback and, 84
  delegating and, 160
  productivity and, 80
  psychological safety and, 79
  resolving conflicts and main-
    taining, 194–195
  universal need for, 81–82
turf wars, 197–205
Tversky, Amos, 104

universal needs, 81–82
Uzzi, Brian, 198–199, 200, 202

value creation, 193–194
values
  alignment with team, 40
  conflicting, designing solu-
    tions for, 94–95
  self-awareness of, 19–20
  shared, in subcultures, 92, 93
virtual collaboration, 175–181
  chemistry in, 15

communication in, 180–181
document sharing for, 177–179
regular meetings for, 176–177
tools for, 33–34
working side by side in, 180
virtual watercoolers, 178–179
voting, clarifying, 173–174
VUCA issues, 70, 75

Watkins, Michael D., 178–179
Webasto, 151–153
Weiss, Jeff, 1–6
Wieber, Frank, 102–103, 104,
  105
Wilson, Tom (executive), 173–174
Winsborough, Dave, 39–45
win-win outcomes, 81, 161–162
Woolf, Jamie, 154, 156, 157–158

Zehner, Deb, 25–35

Notes

Notes

Notes

Notes

Notes

Notes

Smart advice and inspiration from a source you trust.